In Country

Michael Andrews
David Widup

BOMBSHELTER PRESS

Some of these poems have appeared or will appear in the following magazines:

Andrews: *ONTHEBUS, Samisdat Chapbook (A Telegram Unsigned), Lingo, Exquisite Corpse, Voices, The Wormwood Review, The Cathartic, Northeast Journal, The Jacaranda Review* and *Poetry/LA*.

Widup: *ONTHEBUS, Another Chicago Magazine, Voices, Icarus Review*.

© 1994 Michael Andrews & David Widup
First Edition

All rights reserved. Printed in the United States of America. No part of this book may be used or reproduced in any manner without permission from the publisher except in the case of brief quotations in critical articles and reviews.

Library of Congress Catalog Number: 93-072761
ISBN 0-941017-28-1

BOMBSHELTER PRESS
1092 Loma Drive, Hermosa Beach, CA 90254

CONTENTS

INTRODUCTIONS
99% Pacified . . . . Andrews . . 8
In My Bones . . . . Widup . . 11

THE WORLD BEFORE THE NAM
At The Dawn Of The Nuclear Age . . . . Andrews . . 13
I Had No Idea . . . . Widup . . 14
THE FAT MAN . . . . Andrews . . 15
GRADUATION DAY . . . . Widup . . 16
SPUTNIK . . . . Andrews . . 18
18 SEPT. 1968 . . . . Widup . . 19
GUNS & CRUTCHES . . . . Andrews . . 22
RAINBOW . . . . Widup . . 23
THE DRAGON LADY AND THE NUN . . . . . Andrews . . 25
ORDERS . . . . Widup . . 26
THE DRAFT EXAM . . . . Andrews . . 28
RED HORSE . . . . Widup . . 29

IN COUNTRY
Black And White . . . . Widup . . 32
Fng . . . . Andrews . . 33
INCOMING . . . . Widup . . 34
THE OLD HAND . . . . Andrews . . 36
The Nam . . . . Andrews . . 37
MR. TRI . . . . Andrews . . 38
VICTOR DUMMICK . . . . Andrews . . 40
SEXUAL HOLOCAUST . . . . Andrews . . 42
SGT. BIGELOW . . . . Widup . . 43
WAR IS HELL . . . . Andrews . . 44
THE LONG BINH TRAIL . . . . Andrews . . 48
99% PACIFIED . . . . Andrews . . 51
Hong Kong R&R . . . . Andrews . . 53
KOWLOON TO HONG KONG . . . . Andrews . . 54
SHOOTOUT AT THE CERCLE SPORTIF . . . . Andrews . . 55
DYSENTERY I . . . . Andrews . . 57
DOUGHNUTS . . . . Widup . . 58
AN EMPTY MAILBOX . . . . Widup . . 60
MINNIE AND MICKIE . . . . Andrews . . 61
TEA GARDEN GIRLS . . . . Widup . . 62
CHILD BEGGAR . . . . Andrews . . 63
REVOLUTIONARIES IN NAM . . . . Widup . . 65
BOQI . . . . Andrews . . 66
THE PICTURE SHOW . . . . Widup . . 68
COFFIN LUMBER . . . . Andrews . . 69

THE POET'S HEART	Widup	71
CAO DAI TEMPLE	Andrews	72
MY MAMA SAN	Widup	73
CENTRAL MARKET AND THE WORM DOCTOR	Andrews	76
FLO AND THE CYCLO RIDE	Andrews	77
ON THE PERIMETER	Widup	79
YOU CAN SEE BY MY OUTFIT THAT I AM A GRUNT	Andrews	80
SANDY	Widup	81
THE GECKO AND THE BEANIE WEANIES	Andrews	83
FLARES, TRUTH AND THE COLD BLACK NIGHT	Andrews	85
THE BLACK TIGER	Widup	89
HOME LEAVE	Andrews	90
A STOLEN MOMENT	Widup	93
CO TRINH WATCHES FROM THE TREES	Andrews	95
FLO'S PEE AND THE NEARLY DEAD	Andrews	97
THE FREEZING SWEATS	Andrews	98
THE EGRET	Widup	100
THE XTIAN MONTAGNARD	Andrews	101
STARING AT THE MAP	Widup	109
CHOPPERS	Andrews	110
THE TIGER CAGES OF CON SON ISLAND	Andrews	111
UGLY PUSSY	Widup	115
BODY COUNTS	Andrews	116
THE FISH AND I	Widup	120
DEAR JOHN	Widup	121

SHORT TIMERS

Short Timer	Widup	124
STARS & STRIPES	Andrews	125
LAOS	Widup	126
JERRY TABASKI LEAVES TOWN	Andrews	127
READING THE LAMPOON	Andrews	129
BUYING BALLOONS	Andrews	132
XMAS GOES TO WAR	Andrews	133
THE MISSING GUNS	Widup	135
WILLY PETER	Andrews	139
THE ROOT CANAL	Andrews	140
ROCK 'N ROLL WAR	Andrews	144
THE BUNKERS	Widup	146
TIES	Andrews	147
OATMEAL COOKIES	Andrews	150
THE FIRE ANT OFFENSIVE	Andrews	152
AERIAL PORT	Widup	154
BODY BAGS	Andrews	156

IN THE WORLD

Back In The World	Andrews	160
Coming Home	Widup	161
DRYING OUT	Andrews	162
PEACE CORPS PRINCESS	Andrews	163
Looking Back	Andrews	165
WHAT I LIKE, WHAT I CAN WHAT IS EASY AND WHAT IS HARD	Andrews	167
THE BOYS	Widup	169
THE PLACE WE ARE AT LOOKS LIKE HOME BUT I WAKE UP IN THE MORNING AND THE SHOES DON'T FIT	Andrews	172
BACK IN THE WORLD	Widup	173
THE POW'S SITCOM	Andrews	175
THE BARRACKS	Widup	177
4DAY TIRE STORE	Andrews	178
COMBAT BOOTS	Widup	179
PATCHES	Widup	180
BETWEEN A PIG AND A BABY	Andrews	184
WHISPERING AT THE WALL	Widup	187
WARS, BLOODY WARS	Widup	188
THINGS THAT BREAK	Andrews	189

TO THOSE WHO WERE THERE
AND TO THOSE WHO TRIED TO STOP IT

INTRODUCTIONS

99% PACIFIED   MICHAEL ANDREWS

> "...it is important to remember, to spell the names correctly, to know the provinces, before we are persuaded that none of it happened, that none of us were in such places."
>
> **Gloria Emerson, Winners and Loosers**

This is Saigon, 1969 to 1971. It is not Vietnam from the footsoldier's point of view, but from the perspective of a civilian working and dying in the mortal chaos of Saigon. It is certainly not about the colonels, generals, spies, ambassadors, presidents and other such riff-raff that historians automatically tag as Important Persons. Not only is it a false theory that such human debris create history but they are almost exclusively, in my experience, idiots. And dangerous idiots to boot.

There was a very large population of civilians in the Nam, 350,000 from 1965 to 1973. There are no stories about their lives; there is no acknowledgement of their work, suffering, and insanity; they have no clubs, associations, Federal or private assistance or any other kind of benefit. They received no medals, have no Wall, and aside from the journalists who are always willing to massage one another with press coverage, they are rarely written about. They could not collect unemployment. They got no parade, no indictment, no forgiveness and no welcome home. And yet, on a lesser scale, they were exposed to the same war, bullets, bombs, death, Agent Orange and post traumatic syndrome as the military and indigenous population were. They were there to do all the work that the military is incapable of—that is everything but murder.

On 16 January 1969 I got on the big silver bird for Vietnam. It was raining. Noah would have been impressed. I was younger than anyone I have ever known. In a sense, I was not even me. In fact I died in Vietnam. Another Michael was born; smarter, tougher, sadder, different.

No one is born at some particular moment. We die and are born each particular moment by moment. But some moments are bigger, last longer and bite deeper. I was born in Saigon and my life became a new thing. It changed fast and hard and, sometimes, I didn't know it was happening. It took me ten years to look back.

When I did, I cried.

This is a story about a war, two peoples, a place called Vietnam, a cast of characters, and me.

Mostly this is a book about War and its related subsets of cultural insanity. Naturally it includes soldiers and civilians, both the rapists and the victims. It is a story which I have been contemplating for over twenty years. It is a personal matter—it is a matter of burying ghosts.

In the Nam I was stuck in the middle. GIs were dying like flies all around me. The Medivacs flying into 3rd Field Hospital unloaded the meat, living or dead, and hosed down the cement pad. I could understand how they hated an enemy they never saw, shot old women and children, raped, burned, pillaged, and killed their own incompetent leaders. I knew all about male bonding and hunting packs. My guts rumbled with the anger and the Fear, capital F, as constant as death and taxes, and the garbage that drools from the lips of colonels, generals and ambassadors. These are deeply pathological men.

But I was a civilian. I talked to Vietnamese. Some of them were friends of mine. I saw the rape of a culture. I saw an entire matrix of religion, language, education, economics, social fabric, family structure and way of life rattle its last breath, roll over, die and resurrect itself as a caricature imitation of Western culture, vicious and cruel and gobbling up the world. I saw people who were not gooks, slants, slopes, or dinks, but just people like any three-year-old starve to death; ten-year-olds beaten; and sixteen-year-old girls who should have been plucking daisies and playing look-but-don't-touch with the boys become whores with scalpels for eyes and a hard used sixty in just five years of social service.

It was a war of cultures. One of the cultures was Vietnamese. The other was the USA and Saigon. Saigon was a US sub-culture based on class. In essence no culture is based on geography, but on borders that are often economic. Saigon was an upper middle class and elite culture based on the business of war profiteering. And business was good.

The Vietnamese lost all the battles and won the war. They proved that no one can beat a guerrilla army. The only and final solution to a guerrilla war is genocide. That is the solution the generals wanted the USA to deploy. As the economic fantasies of the free market pyramid scheme fail globally, as population continues to explode, as resources dwindle, genocide will indeed become the solution—sooner or later.

In their attempt to survive, the Vietnamese killed their culture. It has gone the way of Aborigines and Eskimos.

The USA also died. It went bankrupt. But it did continue to spread its monocultural fungus into Asia. Communism, they say, is dead. The world monoculture is the sad fact. The earth is a barrel full of fish waiting for the gun. The only culture left is the Corporate culture, disguised as free market democracy. It is not free. It is not a market. It is certainly not a democracy. It is a cultural fungus that is the natural outgrowth of population explosions and not enough rice.

It's just the way things go—not good, not bad.

The overwhelming fact for the American in Vietnam was isolation. For the grunt, the generals and for the civilians there was no more team, no common cause or fellowship—there was only survival.

And there was alone. No matter how many friends die to cover your backside, when you die, you die alone.

What makes alone so awesome are those few moments when a human being is almost not alone. But survival and fear stick their tongues in your ear and whisper, "You ought to know better."

The observable outcome of this is that no one who was in Vietnam, military or civilian, for any appreciable length of time came out untouched. Every one of us was changed to one degree or another. Changed forever. Call it used. Call it rape. It was the experience of a pile of leaves in a hurricane. No one could change a thing. No one had the power. No one got out alive.

We are the fringe people. We live in that pale, cultural no-man's land on the edge of the abyss. The edge demarcates the abyss from the main line culture junkie; the eight to fiver, the mortgaged family man with dog and Chevrolet. In the abyss is hard core death and smack, alcohol and crack, insanity and crime. Often we are expatriates strung out in foreign lands because we can't live here and we can't live in the abyss and we can't stand being on the edge and if the foreign employment dries up we suffer and if we can, we come home and suffer more.

A polite name for us in Vietnamese is My, beautiful—we are the beautiful people.

2,800,000 grunts saw the end of the male myth. 350,000 civilians witnessed the logical conclusion of free market rapaciousness. Many of these people are not admirable. Many are just totalled up under the column labeled "lost souls." Many never knew what hit them. Most of them have managed only survival. More grunts have committed suicide, or died of Agent Orange than were killed in the bush. One out of three are divorced. One out of two are on drugs or alcohol. The best that can said is that some of them managed a peace with themselves, even a dignity. Others only managed the compromises of rationalization. The least that can be said of most is that they were victims, and they kept on breathing.

Shortly after the United States of America died in the Tet Offensive of 1968, I worked as a programmer-analyst for Control Data Corporation, who had a contract with CORDS/MACV, who worked for the U.S. military industrial complex. I worked on a program called Phoenix, whose job it was to assassinate Vietnamese civilians without proof or trial. Naturally, being the military, it was mostly incompetence and bluff, but they did manage to get rid of a few children and some village chiefs who showed a propensity to think for themselves.

We had another system called HES. That stood for Hamlet Evaluation System. It totalled up all the Friendly Hamlets, all the Unfriendly Hamlets, and all the Unknown Hamlets and did a lot fancy arithmetic. In the end it spit out a piece of paper that would say something like "89% Pacified."

One day, the evil emperor Nguyen Van Thieu needed a new Cadillac and a larger Swiss Bank account. Since such wealth was only acquired by convincing the electorate that we were winning a righteous war, and since the only way we could ever win such a war was in the computer, he called the great chief, Tricky Dick, who called his generals, who called MACV, who called a Colonel, who called the CDC Project Manager, who called the chief of programmers, who called my boss, who called me. It seems that Nguyen thought that 89% Pacified wasn't good enough to win hearts and minds. So we threw a switch in a program and counted all the Unknown hamlets as Friendly.

Overnight, Vietnam was 99% pacified.

IN MY BONES
DAVID WIDUP

I can't remember what it feels like to not have the war in my bones. When I think back on my high school days, it's like looking at a story book. I recognize the people and faces - me, Dad, Cec, Sherron, Mike, Kathy - and the events like Graduation Day, my last day at the plastic bottle factory, my trip to Tennessee the week before I went into the service, even Boot Camp. I recognize them all, but I can't feel me in them. It's like I never had an existence before the war. And now I carry it with me wherever I go, all the time.

It's really bad when I'm tired. I'm afraid to be tired, because when I get tired is when I get blown away. I don't see the things I need to see. I forget to watch where I put my boots down. I don't see that small flash ten clicks out. I miss the glance of a old native woman as she passes by, black teeth, black hair, black pajamas, black death. I have woken up afraid almost every morning since I went to Vietnam over 25 years ago. There have been years when the only time I've slept well was when I was drunk or stoned. Hung over and coming down is much, much better than scared to death of a monster that looks just like me.

I was in country for a year beginning in September 1969. I didn't eat for the first six weeks. I couldn't keep food down. I was on duty every night from an hour and a half before sunset to an hour and a half after sunrise. About 14 hours—every night. Sometimes, I'd be sent out with a small construction crew to an outpost. I'd be responsible for securing the construction area around the clock. If it was hot in the area, we'd go four or five days without sleeping. I gave up booze my first week there and just smoked—cigarettes all the time and dope when I felt it was safe. I sold my booze ration to the lifers and used the money to buy dope. Money for nothin.........drugs for free.

I remember many times being struck by the beauty of Vietnam - the blue, warm sheen of the South China Sea; the black sky highlighted by a huge moon, laying low on the runway, some nights it looked as big as a rising sun; the mountains just west of Phan Rang, dense green with trees and ferns. I swear, I could hear the VC in the sound of the wind in those trees. It was a beautiful country, sometimes quiet and calm unlike any place I've ever been.

I was happy there. I learned the fine art of denial and deflection—how to suppress every fear. Fine tuned senses never let me down. I was a happy, self sufficient animal. The longer I was there, the happier I was. Until the end, when I faced into leaving. Then all the horrors I had seen and done, all the overwhelming fears and anger began to pour out of me. It took most of my energy for the next decade to manage the streams of filth and degradation that ran out like rivers in hell. Post Traumatic Stress Syndrome (PTSS) is about the horror of trying to heal while the months in hell play out almost visually, like shapes in an early morning, foggy playground. I remember my first anxiety attack. It was in 1978 after seeing *Coming Home*. I was paralyzed—stuck in my movie seat for what seemed like hours. I didn't sleep for days. My hands shook. At night, in bed, my whole body shook so bad I had to get up and lay on the living room sofa. I remember the feel of the fabric pattern on my skin and how it felt cold and unwilling. It was dark green. I hated it.

Vietnam was not like *Apocalypse Now*. I have never read a poem, read a story, or seen a movie that tells what it was like to be there. Many are true as impressions, but they are false in tone, fact and mood. Others are lacking in the details, the specifics. And I know why. It is those details that pull the trigger that drag us back into hell. It takes a crazy person to pull them out like a rotted skeleton and put them on a page and make them real again—for all the world to see and smell. I have made myself sick writing about Vietnam. And I haven't even started. Not really.

April 13, 1993

THE WORLD
BEFORE THE NAM

MICHAEL ANDREWS
AT THE DAWN OF THE NUCLEAR AGE

If you examine stories about the Nam, or even war in general, the ones that ring true are always made of a lot of little stories, vignettes and episodes. I think that this is so because the big story is always the same—that war kills everything it touches; bodies, spirits, minds, cultures, and economies.

When we tell about Vietnam we often include all that follows right up to this very moment, because it seems to us that all that follows Nam is touched by the same finger that touched us. It is as though we were born in the Nam and that our story is the story of the children of war.

We often tell about Vietnam starting from our births because we sense that there is something unique about our generation. That unusual quality is more than just the baby boom—as a generation we were born innocent and we will die cynical.

This is different from the generations before and after ours. My parent's was the last generation to be born innocent and to live out their lives in the fulfillment of the American Dream. They believed that the American way was not only right, but good. Setting aside the great depression they lived lives of unprecedented luxury and security, and actually achieved something called retirement.

The baby boomers were born innocent also, even though it was under the cloud of World War II. Our youth was played out in the 50's and early 60's, the apex of the American culture. Even now we listen to the music of Buddy Holly and recall paradise. We came into adulthood in the 60's, the decade that was the death of America. The corporate world began to dismantle Democracy. JFK was assassinated. The economy was threatened by military spending and the cold war. Vietnam. Civil rights. The economy was finally broken in the Nam. The Tet offensive broke our spirit forever, and serves in my mind as the killing thrust of the American dream. We knew we were no longer good. We knew we were no longer right. We knew we were no longer innocent. We killed Martin Luther King. We killed Robert Kennedy. We landed on the moon. We elected Nixon. And still we fought the good fight—still believing that we could be right and good and innocent.

By the 80's and Reagan we knew we had lost that battle too. American wealth, right, goodness and innocence were lost forever. Democracy was the cheapest kind of PR trick. The cultural machine crushed us as easily as an elephant tap dancing on an egg. We gave up hope, accepted impotence and defaulted to egocentric fulfillments. We experienced a failure of nerve and lapsed into moral apathy. We became cynics.

The generations following us were born cynics. Innocence is not something that comes with birth in America anymore.

What made our generation unique was more than the accident of the historical moment of the death of America, but the fact that we underwent the transformation from innocents to cynics. We were a generation of Kafkaesque bugs.

And that is what made us great, the 60's great—we tried. We fought the good fight and for a brief while, we won. We forced Nixon out of Vietnam and then out of office. We battered down the walls of racism. The music was great because were we united in a cause, the last gasp of American democracy and freedom. We failed to even notice the great enemy—the corporate world and its pseudo-philosophy of free market buccaneering. In the end it just bought us out and America died.

The following generations merely acquiesced to the dismantling of America, became de-educated and sold their birthright for a polyester suit. Still, we look back to cars with fins, listen to Buddy Holly and the Beach Boys, and even though we are sad, we often wear a secret smile.

I HAD NO IDEA

DAVID WIDUP

The day my Mom died was the beginning of my journey to Vietnam. She died alone, in her bed on a hot July afternoon in 1967. It was the summer between my Junior and Senior year of High School. She was in Rockaway, New Jersey, in a suburban house without air conditioning. I was working in a book bindery in North Manchester, Indiana. We were both sweating at 3:30 PM when she let out her last breath.

If she had lived, I never would have gone to Nam. She hated the war. She loved me. I listened to her. When she died, I lost my Mom, my best friend and only confidant. I had run away that summer - I'm not sure from what. I never thought it would kill her. My brother found her that afternoon and called Dad, who was at work. I can't get the image of her - pale face with gray black hair spilling onto the white pillow, eyes barely shut and lips slightly apart - out of my mind. I cannot separate my going to Vietnam from her death.

I joined the Air Force; it seemed the safest thing to do. I had no idea that they would give me a gun and send me to Vietnam within a year. I had no idea that I would have been better off in the Army or Navy. I had no idea that at 18, I would be put in charge of a small armory and security for 400 men and $25 million of construction equipment. I had no idea, that day Mom died as I looked up at the clock on the shipping dock wall, that from that instant, my life would change. If I knew then what the next two years would hold, I probably would have killed myself.

THE FAT MAN
1945

Before they dropped it on Nagasaki
they signed their names
as though it was an object of art.
They put their wives and children's names on it
as though it were a gift.
On 8 August 1945 they dropped
it out of a B-29 Box Car
and killed 125,000 humans.
They merely injured another 150,000.
A few year later Klaus Fuchs,
a physicist in need of a vacation
and a Swiss Bank account
sold atom bomb secrets to the Soviets.

In school the siren screamed
and we had to crawl under the desk
to avoid the flying glass.
Flying glass seemed like the least
of our worries if our eyes
melted down our cheeks.

For every Einstein, we learn
there are a thousand Oppenheimers.

We are the bomb babies.

We know how the world ends.
It has nothing to do with a whimper.

GRADUATION DAY

As we walk
through the halls
from the gym
onto the football field
the school seems
foreign to me,
like I'd never
been there before.
I notice the lockers
are grey,
the linoleum floor green
and the ceiling white.
I'm wearing long black slacks
and a new white shirt
under my graduation gown.
Some of the boys
have nothing on
under their gowns.
I think of the girls
naked under the soft
black material.
It's over 95 degrees outside,
the sky is clean blue,
clouds lost float and spill,
the sun is hot hot.
We are all sweating,
even before we get outside.
Sitting in folding chairs
on the football field,
the principal tells us
we're the best class
he's ever had,
the class of '68.
The valedictorian,
says that we can
make a difference,
change the world.
I see her the night
she got so drunk
she couldn't stand up,
I took her home,
driving the dark roads
and I walked her down
the long sidewalk,
the outside light

turned on yellow
as we get to the door,
her father calls me a bum,
I'll hear from the police
if anything is really wrong,
you know what I mean, kid?!?,
I hadn't even been with her,
I just drove her home.
In the hot
Graduation Day sun
I hear her end by saying,
"We can make a difference.
We can stop Vietnam.
We can make a better
life for our children."

SPUTNIK
OCTOBER 1957

In 1954 the citizens of these United States bought a war.
The boys in the board rooms and the good Senator McCarthy
couldn't let Ho Chi Minh get away with a happy Vietnam
so we paid the French to pillage, rape and burn.
We pay 78% of France's expense in Nam
and the French give us Dien Bien Phu
where the Viet Minh hiked the cannons up the cliffs
on their back and dug them into the mountain,
shelled and starved the French into submission
then ran them over in a human wave.

Ike wants the tin and tungsten in Nam.
They want the slaves and they want the market.
They want the rubber and they want the trees.
They want the spices and they want the rice.
They want the oil and they want the fish.
They want their minds and they want their votes.
So Ike takes over the job of pillage, rape and burn.

There is trouble in China and there is trouble in Cuba.
Everyone we want to plunder is getting ideas.
We don't like the idea of ideas.

Then the evil empire launches the Sputnik.
It is nothing but a tin can in orbit
but now we know we are only second best.
Now we know that the Russians are smarter than us.
Now we know that men can go to the stars
and that those men won't be straight shooting,
clear eyed, stand talling Americans.

When it gets dark the whole neighborhood
stands out in the street and we watch
the sky for the star that moves fast
and doesn't fall down.

We watch in dumb silence.
We aren't sure what it means
but we sense that something
has changed forever.

Then we go inside, turn on the tube
and watch Harriet jerk Ozzie's chain.

DAVID WIDUP

18 SEPT. 1968

My father wakes me up
at 5:00 AM.
I can smell that
he's already
showered and shaved.
I wonder again
at how he never seems to sleep.

It's grey light
outside my window.
I hear the birds
and a car
every minute or so.
I get out of bed
like a dead man
rising from the grave.

My father drives me to Newark,
to the Armed Forces Induction Center.
We don't talk
as the familiar passes by,
yellow school buses
with black lettering
moving quick to
their first pick up,
High School kids,
smoking cigarettes,
laughing,
even though the day
hasn't yet begun.
I know,
I know nothing,
nothing at all.
I light another cigarette.

My father listens
to classical music
as we drive
Route 46 East.
His uniform fits him well,
I wonder about
the ribbons on his chest.
He is very quiet.
He has been retired
eight years now.

DAVID WIDUP

I was prouder of him
when he wore a uniform
every day,
though I would never
tell him that.

My father swears me in.
We stand as a group,
thirty or forty
young men in jeans
and long hair,
and pledge to
love, honor and obey.
He carries me across the threshold
tired and confused,
me just tired.
He looks at me
as he administers
the time honored oath
to serve, honor, protect,
he looks at me
as if he's never seen me before.
I'm tired.
I don't know
if this is a bad joke,
a nightmare
or another beginning.
I pinch my inner thigh,
it must be for real.

My father is in my thoughts,
his steel eyes wet
as he stares at me
being inducted,
as I get another physical,
strange men
squeezing my balls,
putting their middle finger
up my asshole
too far,
for too long.
I wonder if he knows
this is happening
to his oldest son,
I wonder if he cares.
My father is gone
from my thoughts

late that night,
standing in a spotlight
with 79 new companions.
They are quiet at last,
shifting from foot to foot.
I'm sweating, even though
it's getting cold now.
The first thing I hear
from my Drill Sergeant,
I hear before I can see
his black face
under a dark olive Smoky the Bear hat,
above a facade of starched khakis is:
"LISTEN UP MOTHERFUCKERS.
WHAT I'M ABOUT TO TELL YOU
MAY SAVE YOUR ASS
IN VIET NAM SOMEDAY!"

MICHAEL ANDREWS

GUNS & CRUTCHES
1954-1968

      po• et: *from Greek poietes, "maker," poet from poiein, to make, create.*

My brother Rick and I have cap pistols,
squirt guns, ping-pong ball guns,
pellet guns and BB guns—
22s, 38s, 30-30s, shotguns
and I hobble on the crutches
until the doctors turn me loose
but they still won't let me
play football or run track
and I hang around on the bars
like the school monkey.

When the draft board sends us greetings
Dean and Lance go into the Guard—
Camp Roberts in the summer
and the Watts riots in season.

Rick draws the Nam and more guns
than a Republican ever dreamed.

In the end the crutches save me
from authority, bad education,
brainwashing, the army and death.

I hobbled after life and eventually,
life caught up with me.
The crutches turned to pens and cameras,
mallets and computers
and I became a maker.

With the guns we slaughtered tin cans,
but as far as I know
guns never saved anyone
from much of anything.

And in the end, every gun becomes a crutch.

RAINBOW

Rainbow, Rainbow,
Don't be blue.
Four more years
And you'll be through

From the second floor
bay window
of my boot camp
tinderbox barracks
I see rainbows —
new recruits
in bright yellow shirts
with sky blue lettering
"U. S. Air Force"
across the chest,
dark blue gym shorts
and black combat boots,
the tops of khaki socks
just barely showing
above boot tops
at mid calf —
rainbows marching
in groups of flights,
four rows of twenty,
here and there
along narrow black asphalt roads
crisscrossing Lackland AFB
in San Antonio, Texas.

It's hot here in late September,
over 95 degrees every afternoon
when the rainbows take P. T.
on the huge brown field
at the center of the
hell
I come to know
as Basic Training.

The marching taunts
of the other flights
stomping by
who had been in hell
longer than my
multi-colored
rag tag group

of new recruits
angered us
into wanting
what we feared the most —
becoming a
nameless
faceless
heartless
part of the
big
green
machine.

At the window looking down,
decades later I wonder how many souls
died on those small, hot asphalt roads.

THE DRAGON LADY AND THE NUN
1960

She was Catholic, of course
and evil as a baby raper—
Madame Nhu, Diem's sister in law,
loved power and money,
she loved to have her picture taken,
and she loved most of all
the chance to squash little people
like sitting in the afternoon sun
smashing ants marching in a column.

For the little people
things were not going so well.
Starvation, torture, jail and death
were about the only civil amenities
a citizen was likely to receive
in return for paying taxes.

The Buddhist nun ate a lifetime of pain.
But in the end it is other
people's pain that breaks us.

On June Third 1960 she finds a busy street
and soaks herself with gasoline.
The fumes make her dizzy
but she looks at the sky one last time,
sits in meditation, closes her eyes
and lights herself up.
She turns into charcoal without a whimper
and her message screams around the world.

The Dragon Lady calls it a barbecue,
paints her finger nails
and beats the servant.

I am fifteen years old this summer,
still trying to put an erection to some use.
The pictures of the Dragon Lady
remind me of Snow White's evil stepmother—
nasty in black and mean in sexy.

I go to Hermosa Beach
hunting for bikinis—
the image of the nun
imprinted on my sperm.

ORDERS

April in Altus, Oklahoma
can be hot.
The air conditioned hospital
where I'm temporarily assigned,
smells like antiseptic
and is very, very cold.
I wore winter dress blues
to work every day
until my C.O. ordered me
to get with the program.
In my summer khakis,
short sleeves
and lightweight pants
I freeze.
Sometimes, my whole body shakes.
I go outside to smoke,
stand in the sun
every chance I get.
I think the sun
into my bones
warming,
cleansing.
I'm standing in the sun,
in the large framed doorway
by the back dock
smoking Winstons
and drinking coffee
from a paper cup
when Hindy walks out
towards his new white Mustang
and tells me he heard
I'm going to Nam -
Red Horse, he says -
as he walks by.
I smile,
Hindy's such a card.

A few minutes later,
my C.O. comes out,
hands me the orders
and walks away without a word.
Reading them,
I start to shake,
like I'm inside again,
I look at the sun

surprised to see it still there.
It's finally happening.
I think,
It's finally happening.

THE DRAFT EXAM

When I graduated from High School I was a lost soul.
I knew that the women and the best schools
and the football glory and the new cars were all for
some privileged class of superior beings
to which I did not belong.
One day I get a letter from the draft board.
They invite me to an examination on such and such a day.
Death is no excuse.
And so, on the appointed day,
I go with various friends to downtown L.A.
We line up naked in icy hallways
waiting to have our ears tested.
When we have to pee into a tube
the weird kid sits on the toilet to pee
and the asshole sergeant screams in his face,
"We're all men here. We stand up to piss."
A few queers, or maybe really smart guys,
parade around proudly in lipstick and bras.
They get out the door fast, but the sergeants make
the hermaphrodite line up with the rest of us
to have his ass punched by the sadist with
the plastic gloves, Vaseline and the frozen fingers.
When they read my chart they X-ray my legs
and while I wait they examine
the X-ray of a kid with a steel plate in his head
and the doctors agree that he wouldn't live long enough
to vote, and maybe they could send him home.

That summer JFK is still asking us
what we can do for our country.
No one gives a shit about telling us
what we can do for ourselves.

I never knew that you could see a picture of death
in black and white, and they joke about the kid
and look at my X-ray and stamp me 4F—
damaged goods—and the good doctor hands
me his card and says, "Look me up
when you're ready to have your hips replaced."

RED HORSE

Rapid
Equipment
Deployment

Heavy
Operational
Re-supply -
Squadron of
Engineers

Red Horse.
Formed by the same Act of Congress
as the Green Berets.
For the same purpose.
Killing people more efficiently.

We could build a bridge,
extend a runway,
repair a communication tower,
lay down an AM-2 matting chopper pad,
fix a perimeter, barbed wire and all,
put up a bomb shelter,
faster,
better,
than anyone in the world.

We were stronger,
could drink more,
sleep less,
work harder,
than anyone in the world.

Red Horse.

Red Horse training is at
Eglin Air Force Base, Florida
Field #2.
I get off the plane at 8 PM
in July
and I'm sweating so bad
I'm wet from head to toe.
The first thing I hear is
"You think this is bad,
wait till your ass is in Vietnam!"
I rethink the merits of joining the Air Force

so that they don't give me a gun
and send me to Vietnam.

For eight weeks,
I learn how to kill, maim and brutalize.
It's hotter than I can ever remember being.
At night,
I lay naked on my cot in the open bay barracks
or bed roll in the field tent
and think about stars
and my dead Mother
and sex with women
I don't even know.
I fall asleep.

Two hundred of us
sweat through Florida's hottest summer
in one hundred years
thinking that hell is hotter yet.
At the Golden Coast club,
I'm picked up by an 18 year old girl,
decades younger than me, it seems,
and wake up on the beach naked beside her
the next morning.

Red Horse.
We flew from Florida
to Alaska
to Tokyo, Japan
in a very short eternity
in the belly of a C-141.

Red Horse.
All the training
and discipline
and muscles
counted for the cube root of fuck all
when that plane nose dived
into hell.

IN COUNTRY

BLACK AND WHITE   DAVID WIDUP

My image of Nam before I got there was black and white. What I knew was what I had seen on a TV set - black and white. What I thought about the war was good guys, victims all, fighting a miserable, self serving war. Black and white. I remember the Life article one week that had pictures of all the American servicemen killed in Vietnam in the past week. Black and white pictures.

    I can remember every hour between when I got orders to go and when we touched down at Bien Hoa. It was five months - two months at Altus AFB, Oklahoma, one month of leave, two months of RED HORSE training at Eglin AFB, Florida. I still remember it all.

    I thought a lot about going to Canada, but never figured out how to do it. Having volunteered for the Air Force, in 1968, in the middle of the War, it felt contrary to desert when Uncle Sam decided it was time for me to go. But, I never thought it would happen. It seemed so unreal, those long, colorful five months from April through September of 1969. I kept thinking that I would wake up from the dream and it would be over. I should have known - the dream was in color and the Nam was black and white.

FNG

MICHAEL ANDREWS

I don't know why I went. By 1964 I had stopped listening to the music. It had become false, concerned only with surfboards, fast cars and adolescent sex. It was ignoring the fact that there was something more serious going on in the world—something serious was wrong. I did not know any of this. I only felt it in the lower intestine. I listened only to classical, Frank Sinatra and Ella Fitzgerald. I built and lived on a boat, then instead of going around the world, I got off to become a monk. Then instead of becoming a monk, I stopped at a lady's house for a year and was saved by sex. By the time I was offered a job in the Nam I had a lot of excellent reasons for going, but I had no good idea of why I was going. Later, I called it the itch. It really doesn't matter—I was there.

I stepped into an airplane at LAX a terrified innocent. In the Nam innocence was called FNG, Fuckin' New Guy. I was green from ears to toes.

I was in love too. Her name was Flo and she had my number so perfectly that it scared me to death. After all, I was a guy who was thinking of becoming a monk. I was also innocent enough to buy into that cultural myth of disinformation called eternal fidelity. But I was afraid, not of war which I should have been, but of human relations, which I should have been. There is a difference between war and human relations. War, in the final analysis has only one lesson to teach—that war is a waste of everything. Human relations teach us almost everything there is to know of value in an unending river of surprises.

In any case, I took the job.

DAVID WIDUP

INCOMING
BIEN HOA

Twenty seven hours in a C-141
with 200 of my closest friends,
stopovers in Anchorage and Tokyo
and a landing like a ride
on the Hurricane roller coaster
at the Steel Pier in Wildwood.

We get off the plane in our stateside fatigues,
looking out of place already.
I pick up my duffel bag.
It feels much heavier than a day ago
when I carried it across the tarmac
at Eglin Air Force Base, Florida.
It's still cool from being at 40,000 feet.
We walk slowly to a long line of tables
with folding chairs under an overhang
at the far end of the aerial port.
There's room for all of us and then some.
It's a short walk from the plane
but the sweat is pouring off my face
long before I get there.
It's 0900 hours.
Once we're all seated,
we in-process.

The sun is high in the sky.
It's a clear blue and there are palm trees
all over the place - it's very green.
War is supposed to be dark and brown,
not sunny and green, I think.
Looking towards the base,
I see oriental people in uniforms,
others in black pajama bottoms
with light, loose fitting blouses
and straw coned shaped hats.
Nobody said anything about Vietnamese on base,
and I'm thinking about good guys and bad guys.
I've got an ache between my temples
that throbs every time my heart beats.
I'm thirsty and want to go to sleep.

The major starts our in-processing
with a long speech

about what we need to remember here,
the rules I'm supposed to know and practice,
the Military Assistance Command - Vietnam
(MACV for short),
Rules of Combat Warfare.
I cannot follow his sentences
from beginning to end.
I start chain smoking to stay awake
and it makes my head pound harder.
I tune out,
but remember hearing that the attack siren
is tested every day at noon
and to be aware that every once in awhile
Charlie lobs a few rockets in
just for fun, knowing we're ignoring the siren.

I fill out many forms,
the only one I remember
is the one that asked me
if I wanted to sign up
for a consecutive tour
in Vietnam or elsewhere
outside the States.
I checked the box marked "no" without thinking.
Only two hours in country
and I'm already longing for home.

THE OLD HAND

The plane burrows into the steam
and hits dirt in the Filipino night.
It is dark and hot and sweat
drips from the light bulbs
in the airport bar.
I sweat with all the dignity
an idiot can muster
wearing a tweed suit in the tropics.
In an hour or two the plane
will haul my naive self to
the Republic of Vietnam.
I drink something cold and sweet
like real men are supposed to do.
The older guy sitting next to me
is dressed in a frayed and crumpled
Hawaiian shirt, baggy pants
and dusty exhaustion.
He just came from the Nam,
going home with his dead eyes,
empty wallet and dying adrenals.
His voice echoes out of a hollow
tunnel, leading to alien landscapes.
We talk civil nonsense until
I find the crack to slip in my
only question, "What's Nam like?"

I can't see what he sees when
he looks at me, first mad, then sad.
He lets out a lungfull of tired breath,
swallows his drink and says,
"It'll grow on you,"
and walks out into the night.

THE NAM MICHAEL ANDREWS

The reason all true stories about the Nam involve hyperbole is because it was so alien a universe that no one who was not there at that time will ever grasp the experience, the smell of it, the feel, the taste, the terror, the moral outrage, the pure out of this universeness of it. It is simply beyond art, language and translation. It is ineffable. It is incommunicable. In our desperation to tell our fellow humans about what had happened in the Republic, in order to communicate the truth of the emotional, psychological, factual and spiritual impact, our stories must dwell on the most intense, the most bizzare, the most horrific—and in pursuit of the reality of it, we are forced to utilize the power of hyperbole, myth, fantasy and the blackest of black, black humor.

MICHAEL ANDREWS

MR. TRI

> "We shall never know how many Vietnamese became 'Americanized,' became tragic victims of cultural imperialism.... Few of us who were there can claim innocence. It is useless now to ask what has happened to the Vietnamese who worked for the Americans... It is not a question of their being punished now. The question is if all of us harmed them and how much."
> **Gloria Emerson, Winners & Losers**

Mr. Tri is fat for a Vietnamese.
He is also kind of ugly,
one eye just a scar of white
rolling back in his head, as though
it can't stand to look out at the world.

He is the computer operator on the midnight shift.
I don't know who he is connected with
or what clout he hefted to get the job
but it is a one in a million job for a Vietnamese—
10 times the wages, plus protection
and his children get to eat every day.

My job is to supervise
and Mr. Tri does all the work.
He hangs the tapes, feeds the cards,
pulls the printouts.
He is a tireless, energetic little butterball,
sweating in the air conditioning
in his T-shirt and thongs.

I call him Mr. Tri.
He calls me Mr. Mike.

We are friends.

Mr. Tri does favors for me,
bits of fruit and tea, little things
he doesn't do for the other Americans.

One night I am trying
to sharpen my folding knife
and seeing that it won't take an edge,
Mr. Tri takes it home with him.
He grinds out the blade on a coarse wheel,
brings it back, ugly, but sharp—
just like Mr. Tri.

All the operators do things for me
because I protect them from the brass
and the racism of the programmers,
so they think of me as a good man.

They are afraid of most Americans.

For good, god damned reasons.

When all the work is done at night
Mr. Tri curls up on the tape shelf
and goes to sleep.
I have a curfew pass
so I take the grease gun
and drive home in the Scout.

We are friends—
Mr. Mike and Mr. Tri.

VICTOR DUMMICK

Victor was a born good guy.
He always rode in a on white horse.
All through our Christian grade school
career he was the Class President.
Victor was one those short guys
that always floated to the power slots,
and being a take-charge kind of guy
Victor was always in charge of everything.
Everything but me. I was a goof on crutches.
That put me just outside the law, and Victor.
One day, on the playground swings,
the game was to swoop down and snatch up
one of my crutches, and when I missed
I yelled, "God Damn it to Hell."
Dead silence pulsed from eight terrified eyes.
"Don't ever let Victor hear you say that"
they all told me, "Victor hates swearing."
Victor loved the rules. He loved the law.
Victor was a great believer in heaven and hell—
a book told him so, and Victor did everything by the book.
Victor never cussed and he made life hell for anyone who did.
He liked things done right, by his book,
and the Right Way was generally His Way.
Victor was a guy on his way to heaven.

15 years later the playground turns to war.
I am sweating away my innocence in Saigon,
burning up calories and naivete
watching guys who play by the rules
get as dead as boiled champagne.
Someone else is always making up the rules.
The people who make up the rules tend
to live long, untroubled lives.

I do not understand a god damn thing,
except that I am sure that I know where hell is.

My mother sends me a letter with a newspaper
clipping about how it was that Victor was
an officer, and no doubt a gentleman,
sailing on a ship bound for the Republic
and how he was lost at sea
and what a great guy he was
and a hero and all.

My mother always thought that Victor
was the perfect little gentleman.
"Dear Mom," I write, "Victor was a prick."
He was a little runt who liked big rules.
When the article says 'Lost at sea'
it means that he turned so many lives
into little cyclones of shit and hell
with rules and right and power and law
that some equally nasty individual
pushed him off the fantail.

It was an act of kindness to shove him off
the fantail rather than just toss him overboard,
because the screws chewed him into
little tiny bits of shark bait
so Victor didn't have to die slow,
five or six days of hell waiting for the sun
to drive him crazy enough
to drink the salt, salt sea.

Victor took the direct route to heaven.

These days, I cherish my little spot in hell
and I am not a stickler for the rules.

MICHAEL ANDREWS

SEXUAL HOLOCAUST

You want to fuck her now and then—
that's a friend and you pay as you go,
ten bucks, a fast suck, a sweaty hump
to explosive decompression and no chat,
just a half smile and you're free to go
and free to come again.
You want to fuck her full-time exclusive—
that's a girlfriend and it is more economical,
free all nighters and kitchen rights.
You want her to move in—
that's a wife and it costs next to nothing
except everything you own
and everything you will ever own
and a certain possibility of nagging
and the sex dries up like iced tea
in a bucket of white hot sand
but when it's time to skip back to the world
you just pack up one morning and catch a plane.
But if you want to take her home to mom—
then it's 50,000 piasters and several months
of the reddest kinds of tape.
You can do it in a week's time for double.
A mere $300 at black market rates
buys an Asian bride
all giggles and spice with the heart
of a cheap calculator and a pussy
that will vibrate a baseball bat to sawdust.

Gone are the days of the cow and a beaded belt.

It is much harder for the gay persuasion
to export a boy, but money will buy any dream
you can afford, or any dream
you have the guts
to die for.

And the sad old men wander from tea bar to hand job
convinced that the sixteen year old whores
love them the way Audrey Hepburn loves Carey Grant
and the sad old men pay the price and take the clap

and when death is ringing your back door bell

there is no such thing as a false dream.

SGT. BIGELOW

After three weeks
at Eglin Air Force Base,
First Sgt. Bigelow,
picks me out of a full squadron formation
and tells me I'll be in charge of Security
once we get to Vietnam.

I'm only 18,
and still learning how to dress,
masturbate
and write a check.

I worry about how my mistakes
will kill somebody,
not just somebody,
but Bill,
who I drink with on Saturday nights
and Schmidty,
who takes all my money at Hearts -
he's got a wife and five girls.

Our first rocket attack,
on day 3 of 365,
I forget to flip the switch
that rings the buzzer to alarm
Sgt. Bigelow
and all the other lifers
of their impending doom.

The next morning,
he yells at me for over an hour,
then hugs me and whispers,
"Don't fuck up again"
in my ear.

I don't.

No matter how drunk or fucked up,
I make sure that Bigelow's ass
is in the bunker come Charlie time.
I learn how to be a child once again.

MICHAEL ANDREWS

WAR IS HELL

"There were always the jokes; it was the safest language to use..."
Gloria Emerson, Winners and Losers

I am riding in a Cyclo.
It is a 3-wheeled monster with 2 seats up front
and in the back a bicycle seat over an unmuffled 2-stroke motor.
It is spitting mountains of smoke all over the street behind us,
dodging deuce-and-a-halfs and Honda 50s.
It costs me a quarter to go downtown Saigon
past Third Field Hospital where the meat choppers
have just come chunking down, belching up
ground GI, body burgers and American goulash.
Everyone is angry at the choppers for stopping traffic,
after all they are either dead, or soon dead,
and the living want to get home or downtown and get on
living and living and living and living.

Bombs and flares and two-stroke motors we rattle
down Cach Mang, over the bridge where it turns into Cong Ly
and where the stink of the river when the tide is low
is 2000 years of garbage and human shit.
We stumble over the beggars, the whores and the smack hustlers
and we try not to step on the dying or the crippled
or the guys with faces that are melting down their shoulders
and we go to Tinh Nam's restaurant and drink the sangria
in the huge crystal punch bowls with whole pineapples
and mangoes and oranges and papayas floating in it
and gobble down foot long lobsters for one thin buck, MPC.
Tom McKenna has just been robbed again.
He gets it about every other month after the parties
with all the whores and the Filipino rock bands
and the cases of whiskey and beer, kilos of grass
and the refugees from pain flood through the night
but this time they came back in broad daylight with shotguns
and M-16s and a no-nonsense attitude and they cleaned out
his cameras and TV and stereo and refrigerator and stove.
Tom raises his sangria and says, "War is hell."

He says that—War is hell—and we laugh
until the tears flood into our crystal punch bowls.
It's our little joke.

We go down to Tudo Street, a thousand Tea Bars
flares in the sky, neon signs and whores whirling
like all the constellations that ever floated through

MICHAEL ANDREWS

the heavens that our sad little dreams told us
were just around the corner.
We fight it out with the taxi driver in the big, black Citroen
1935 style, when they still covered the upholstery with human skin
and headlights sat up on the tops of fenders
the way god meant for headlights to be.
What the hell, he must have a family to feed and children to bury.
We tip him enough to be generous without spoiling him
for the next guy and to keep down the inflation which is
starving half the city and makes the whores put on airs.

We go in a bar as black as the night we are trying to hide from,
a place where dreams come true if you dare to dream at all
and where the ladies with the golden hearts come out to play
where we are all vampires, coming out at night
and where we never look in mirrors.
We don't talk about death or fear or war or hate or right or wrong.
It's against the rules; a matter of bad taste to mention
starvation and rape and bullets and torture and tears.
We are all waiting for Tet instead.
It is fair to say that everyone is nervous since last year when
the Cong nearly pushed us into the sea and took the Embassy
and overran Hue and Dak To and killed everything in sight
sweeping through Gia Dinh where I live now, near the airport
in the big concrete USAID building where they say that all
the crazy fucking American civilians ran berserk with fear
ran amok with all their guns shooting one another
and their maids and down into the streets because they were
that shit-faced scared, John Wayne-ing it till the Cong ran them out.
Everyone is afraid to live there now except us new guys
who don't mind because the rent is so cheap when everyone else is
dying and dying and dying and dying.

We do not talk about dying. It is not the thing to do.
They say instead that Charlie blew his wad last Tet,
that he has nothing left, that there is no sweat this year.
Everyone sweats in the steam in the night in the bar in the dreams
thick and sweet and sad
and I think about my 9mm grease-gun, Swiss made
and places to run and places to hide
and will I shit my drawers when the shit hits the fan.

The girls float around us like all the dreams of all the perverts
since the first Neanderthal got his knuckles slapped.
Her hair is a black waterfall of night and calligrapher's ink
and she sits in my lap and casually drops her hand to the ticklish
part of my thigh and says, "Hello hippy boy, how long you be Vietnam?

45

MICHAEL ANDREWS

You have wife? Girlfriend maybe? You buy me tea?
You want girlfriend make you so much too happy?
I marry you we go away be so happy so many nights."
And that's how innocent we are—
it only takes a dream that simple to make us cry. Impossible dreams.
Cheap dreams, cheap at any price, dreams to take the night away.
I tell her that I have a girl in the world and I can't marry her.
She says, "What amattah you cherry boy? You like little boys maybe?"
"No," I say, "I like you"—and that's the rock bottom truth.

You have to understand Vietnamese sunsets
to get the picture of her mouth
all magenta and salmon and orange and billowing in the wind—
and you have to think about dusk in Saigon when the color bleeds away
and there is just enough light to see
just enough light to get fooled
just enough light to see the things you want to be there
to see the things you are afraid might be there
and that's the color of her skin, dusky—
and just before the night goes black someone shoots up some flares
little suns washing away the stars because
we are afraid of skies that are that dark
and those are her eyes—
and she smiles like all the Buddhas that ever promised heavens
and lifts her long, thin thigh out of her miniskirt
and puts her small hand where I ache and I am hard
and she puts her tongue in my ear and moans
and we don't talk about dying or starvation or fear or
what we do not see in the mirror or bullets or Tet or
what can happen in the nights that are that black
and I run my hand down her thigh to where her panties are all wet
and no one mentions the frag that almost killed us all
or the black hole full of black ice in our stomachs
but someone says that the lobster for a buck is a steal
and that these are the world's most beautiful women
and the wine ain't half bad and the dope is the best anywhere
and someone says, "War is hell," and we all laugh
and we laugh
and we laugh
and we laugh
and we laugh or we die.

She is rubbing furiously at my crotch as if
one orgasm will make all the world a dream.
It's so hard it hurts, her tongue slithering in and out of my ear
and she is moaning when I touch her where no war has ever been
and I say, "War is hell,"

and I throw back my head and laugh

Ha Ha Ha Ha Ha Ha Ha Ha.

Well—I guess
you just had to be there.

MICHAEL ANDREWS

THE LONG BINH TRAIL

I have a brand new Suzuki 50 cc motorcycle—
it's time for high adventure and Mike Petrale,
Wayne Brady and I haul out the maps.
We are going to Long Binh the hard way.
We're not interested in the four lane highway,
we are taking the back roads and the scenic routes.

We can't even find our way out of Saigon
so Petrale stops some kid by a beer-tin shack.
Petrale has told us all about how he can talk Vietnamese.
He babbles on to the kid, who motions us
to follow him down the alley where he shows
us his sister who is a virgin and desperately
wants to get fucked by three Americans,
one at a time or all together, so long as
we can pay the mortgage and feed the chickens.

So much for Petrale's language skills.

I find a road on the map and we plunge
into the boonies. It's only ten miles out
but they say that Charlie owns it.
I wouldn't be surprised. All our side can do
is secure the tea bars and the sit-down toilets.

I stop everywhere in the jungle,
by the rivers, in the rubber plantations
clicking the shutter and horsing
around with the kids.

Children understand war better than you think.
The average Vietnamese ten year old
is more savvy than the whole voting population
of the U.S. — but then, so is a parakeet.

It takes a lot of hours on the back road.
Every now and then some young male
gives us the eyeball, wishing it were night
and he was in his black jammies.

By some coffee and cream river I shoot the plantation.
It is made of beer sheets and has a bridge
across Old Muddy. The kids stand on the veranda
and smile and laugh and wave.
It doesn't take long for a small army of them

to cluster around the bike.

They fool around with my watch,
touch the Levis and stare at themselves in the mirrors.
I take a picture of a boy whose palette
is so badly cleft that there is a canyon
cracking his face in two.

I don't believe any of them has yet
had the opportunity to kill someone.
I don't believe they have a reason to want to.
I snap old papa-san squatting in the weeds.
He smiles and puffs away at his joint.

Mostly everyone is friendly
and mostly I take snaps of the kids.
Two small boys pose on their buffalo cart.
When the shutter slaps closed
they want to be paid with cigarettes.
I give them a few hundred P.
It is nothing to me and a lot
to a kid in the bush.

Taking their pictures is my way
of not letting them break my heart.

The tiny girl has black oceans
in her eyes, staring deep and wide
at my face, until finally she reaches
up a hand no bigger than a small apricot
and runs it along my cheek.
Her mouth is cracked open with concentration
and her eyes follow every motion of my face.
I am the first American she has ever laid eyes on.
Her hair is the shape of a coconut.
Two dimples bracket her smile.
She puts her hand in mine.

We are in love as pure as a mother's milk.

This little girl teaches me
what other guys die for and never learn.
Some guys kill to learn it.
Some guys watch best friends die to learn it.
Some guys become a lifelong bleeding
wound and never learn it.
And when the war stalks us in the night

MICHAEL ANDREWS

and the dreams ambush us in our sleep
some men dream of the face they killed,
or the mutilated face of a best buddy,
or the plea for life in the eyes of a dying man.

I dream of the face of a four year old girl.
She weighs thirty pounds and she
is dressed in rags and barefoot in a jungle.

Her eyes are two black oceans.

She shows me—
        the face of war.

99% PACIFIED

It's 69, Saigon.
I work all night in the computers,
the fluorescent, the air conditioning
go to the Cercle Sportif
the sun sweating uphill
monsoons
falling,
falling—
lift weights upstairs
in an open veranda
sweat falling
like the rainy season
rain muffling
the traffic on Troung Pa.
I go out on the porch—
it is almost like
peace
the rain,
the young girls
riding motorcycles
in their au dais
each one a lotus
floating in a
deep green pond.

It is hot.
I take a shower
in the old tile stall
go to the huge water urn
pour the cold water
down my back
get dressed
drink a citron soda
on the restaurant porch
watching the rain—
walk home
soldiers
small arms fire
barbwire
broken glass.
I carry a 9 mm
for a while
take it off
when I feel silly
and the rains come.

MICHAEL ANDREWS

Tet is over.
The women like bamboo
like asian nights
finger my cock
with one hand
heft gold in the other.
I love them all.
The rains come—
not peace.
It is almost that way
some days
except for all those guys
in plastic bags and out
who never get the beauty
of this rain
or the women
how they survive
all the wars.
They give you peace.
You pay what they ask.

"Hello hippie boy
how long you be Vietnam?"

I smile
take back my cock
leave a little gold
walk home
in the rain.

HONG KONG R&R   MICHAEL ANDREWS

By the time I got my first R&R in Hong Kong I was a haunted man. I had no clue as to the magnitude of my transformation. Physically, I went from mildly out of shape to hard, lean and muscular. Emotionally I went from friendly, easy going and scared to a profoundly deep anger. Politically I went from indifference to anarchist. Ethically I went from live-and-let-live to imperative moral combat. Intellectually I went from innocent naivete to a fundamental cynicism. Spiritually I went from devout submission to Luciferian revolt.

When I stepped off the plane in Hong Kong's Kai Tak airport I had just come from a season in hell to be a tourist in paradise. I loved everything about Honk Kong. I had missed the ocean. I had missed peace.

I was already committed to living my life with Flo and was trying to find a way to get her to Vietnam. I had plans to return to The World in September for a Home Leave. I was faithful, and except for masturbation, celibate. That did present a few trials, temptations and stresses, but I weathered them all. System Development Corporation, my employer had so far not kept their promise to promote me from computer operator to programmer, but claimed it was only a matter of a few months.

Nevertheless, I was exhausted and angry from watching my view of the world disintegrate like a long fade out in a B grade movie.

In Country means only one thing in the Nam—In The Nam. I was essentially a celibate monk in love living in the land of sex come true. It was the most exquisite of mortifications of the flesh. I was an idiot, no doubt about it.

Back in country System Development continued to lie about my promotion. I went in search of another job and easily got hired on at Control Data Corporation as a programmer in October. So, in September I took my home leave, back in The World, back home, Los Angeles California. I was still too much in love and too green to notice any reverse culture shock. Flo and I were busy making plans, getting laid and sleeping in. I did not even notice that I did not talk much to anyone about the Nam. I did not even notice that I already knew instinctually that it could not be done.

Back in country again I went to work for CDC. SDC extorted the expenses of my home leave from me even though I had it coming. I was beginning to form opinions—about war and about corporations.

A few months later I managed to get Flo a job at CDC as a report typist in the very same Quonset that I worked in, at the backside of the little Pentagon, MACV.

In due time, she came to the Nam.

Later, after Flo got to the Nam, we went shopping in Hong Kong. We have been shopping ever since. We assaulted Hong Kong like a horde of parental Santas storming K Mart. Early on sexual joy had died for us. I was angry at the world. Flo was angry at me. She thought I had changed, and for the worse. I did not notice any change, and Flo did not notice that she had also changed. The fortunes of war—and quite probably these two kinds of angry could be the normal culturally induced, genderal response to war. Sexual joy gets reduced to either sexual frenzy or to a sexual ice-age. Nevertheless, we have been in love ever since.

We had only a handful of friends that we found to be decent, intelligent human beings. From this time on I never again believed the human species to be either intelligent, ethical or mature. I never again believed the species to be entirely sane.

We made several trips to Hong Kong. On one of them Jackie and Warner met us there, but usually we were on our own. It is an interesting city in its way, and at the time it was the city I liked best in The World. But in reality it was merely the closest city that wasn't The Nam.

MICHAEL ANDREWS

KOWLOON TO HONG KONG

I cross on the Star Ferry from Kowloon to Hong Kong
white water surging forward at my feet
and the sea, grateful for my return—
black and gray storm clouds billow,
and pillar high above the city.

The island is silent, and waits for rain.

I stink of jungle and death.
The heat and stench of Nam
has plugged my nose with concrete,
carved my eyes into caves
where dragons live.

The city tosses in her bed, dreaming of me.
She steams with lust as long as I am young.
She is as busy as a whore on Saturday night
changing money, sea traffic, buying and selling,
lights and music, taxis and pimps—
she is in the business of dreams come true.

The ocean's dark, menstrual wine sloshes
among the rocks and wharfs, the islands and trees.
Sea-going vessels, lightning and rain,
the night blankets the seething lust of the city.
She nestles into bed, wiggles her fanny, and waits for me.

I am on a hill watching her lights stutter and blink.
I am writing this poem for the city and its sea,

one more night closer to my death.

SHOOTOUT AT THE CERCLE SPORTIF

The first weekend that Flo is in country
I take her to the Cercle Sportif
just to show her that we really are civilized
in Saigon—just because a bunch of wildly
snobbish Frenchmen and even more snotty
Vietnamese millionaires have a sports club.

So Warner and I leave the ladies
elegantly sipping citron sodas on the veranda
and play an hour's worth of steaming hot handball.
When it's over we head back to the lockers,
pausing on the veranda to tell the ladies that
we gentlemen will join them shortly
and we proceed on to the showers and lockers.
Half way there someone is screaming in French,
which I hardly notice because I don't understand
a word of it until someone jerks my arm
and starts screaming in my ear.
I am merely confused because all I can gather
is that he keeps screaming that he is the President
and so I congratulate him and turn to go on
but he grabs me again, shakes his finger
in my face and screams even louder.
Finally, between me and Warner and a whole
flock of Vietnamese we are led to a sign
tacked on the entrance to the showers
that says in French that gentlemen must
always wear shirts and shoes.
No problem with the shoes, but in the
100 degree heat and 99% humidity
I took off my shirt. What the hell,
I'm just a surfer kid form Southern California
and only an idiot, or a Frenchman would
wear a shirt on a day like this.

"Okay," I say, "Sorry. From now on
I'll wear a shirt," and I turn to go
into the showers when the fat Frenchman
grabs me again only this time I shake him off
and grab him by the throat, lifting him
up and back off his feet and I tell
the Vietnamese flunky that translates
to, "Tell the fucking President
that if he ever touches me again
I am going to throw him off the balcony,"

MICHAEL ANDREWS

which he repeats in French while the president
goes from wino red to ghostly white
and I go in and take my shower
while he shouts that I must leave
without a shower immediately
and once again I have it turned into
impeccable French— "Tell the president
to go fuck himself with a pig's dick."

When I finish the shower I gather up Flo
and we get on my 50cc Suzuki
and are mere moments from a clean get away
when we are surrounded by the White Mice
and one little Saigon cop with a 45
aimed at my nose and shaking like
a cheap drunk on three days of strong coffee.

Flo is screaming in my ear, "Stop.
Stop he's going to kill us. Stop Stop Stop."
I don't hear a word because I am too pissed
off and I am revving the motor in preparation
for simply running over the nervous little
gunman, but I am blocked by the huge crowd
and can't really move until the president and his
flunky arrive and demand my membership card
at which news the crowd gasps that
such a barbarian could actually
be a member of the Cercle Sportif
and at that moment the MP's arrive on the back
of a jeep with a 50 caliber at the ready
and the crowd disperses while the president
marches off triumphant, in possession
of the offending membership card.

We ride back to the villa in the traffic
and I am ready for an afternoon of sexual abandon
but Flo is nothing if not stressed out,
and not particularly in the mood having
had to look down the barrel of a 45 at the wrong
end of an individual of unreliable motivations.
I can't get a handle on what has upset her
because I hadn't noticed anything unusual about
the day so far except for a certain lack of sex.

And that's the way things stay.

DYSENTERY 1

It starts in the night, the chocolate squirts
and desperate leaps onto the toilet's saddle
as though I am going to gallop away
to rescue some maiden on a runaway buckboard
but I merely gush out my intestines
until morning comes and it starts coming clear
with the cramps and headaches and nausea
and a fever so high the sweat
can't wait to boil off my skin.

By noon the fever is so high
I start taking showers to cool off
and I stand in the green tile and cool spray
hallucinating and I am sure that I am in the jungle,
in a monsoon waiting for a jungle maiden
with whom I will run away to some
green paradise but then Warner comes in
to check on me at lunch time.
He takes one look, loads me in a taxi
and hauls me down the road to Third Field
Hospital where a world weary medic
hands me the anti-biotics and the usual
instructions before returning
to the traumatic amputees and the malaria folk
and in a few hours I fall into a sweet sleep
and wake up to a solid shit
and a cool green reality.
I am as limp as a dead erection
and it's worth more than an all night girl
just to not feel the sloshing nausea
but I stare at my depressing ceiling
and I miss my jungle maiden.

DOUGHNUTS

My first meal in Vietnam
at a Mess Hall
the size of my High School,
I eat peas and carrots,
mashed potatoes
and sliced mystery meat.
I vomit it all up
on a chopper pad,
hundreds of black winged,
metal spiders clawing at the air.

I don't eat for weeks and weeks.
Strong is gone from me,
I'm shaking cold in the heat,
sweating rivers in the cold.
I have a knife in my belly.
When I think about removing it,
some monster digs it deeper,
and turns it hard into me.
I am afraid.

In October,
Lou Ferrara arrives,
and in November,
he starts baking doughnuts.
A few weeks later,
he stops in the armory,
on his way to bed at 3 AM,
and asks if we want doughnuts.
He has a bag full of them.
The rest eat.
I think of dying
and my dead mother
and the reason why Mars is red and not blue.

The next night,
Lou says
"Eat one, it's good food."
I try one
and return to my dark self.
The next night,
I eat two,
with a cup of coffee.
My pulse, slow and steady,
becomes my friend.

I think about home
for the first time in months.

I eat Lou's doughnuts every night
for weeks and weeks.
I get stronger, I'm awake.
I start cleaning my M-16,
go to base security briefings and try to understand.
I make friends with my guards,
I start to learn Vietnamese.
Doughnuts are my only staple.

Lou goes on R&R in Hawaii,
he meets his wife Di there,
I get sick his first night gone,
and don't eat anything for a week.
He comes back depressed
so all he does is sleep and work.
No more of Lou's doughnuts.
I lose twenty pounds.
I pick a fight with a lifer
and put the barrel of my .38 in his mouth
and pull back the hammer.
Bruce and Jonesy pull me off
just in time.

I drink Jack Daniels' straight
from the bottle at 9 AM
and scowl at the wall.
My empty stomach rebels at the alcohol.
I think about soft skin and red hearts,
worry about being alone,
kick the table over,
curse my headache and my heart,
full of pain, and empty,
and crawl to bed
in the hot, wet daytime.

AN EMPTY MAILBOX

I walk across Bien Hoa slowly,
heading for my mailbox.
I chain smoke Winstons.
I think of the rejection of an empty mailbox,
how my stomach knots,
heart falls,
large and spent,
into the hollow me.
I turn around,
go back to the barracks.
It's easier in the field,
there's no mailbox to be empty there.

Greg Wisher works in the mail building.
He's rich from shipping dope
back to the world.
He tells me when my mail slot is full.
I don't go there otherwise.
But I start the walk
every morning
before I go to sleep.

MINNIE AND MICKIE

Minnie and Mickey
are what the grunts call them.
They don't have real names
and they are brother and sister.
Minnie is 13 and once had a doll.
Mickey is 9 and used to be a child.

The grunts all took Minnie into the bush
for some quick pussy
and Mickey ran errands,
cleaned weapons, shined boots
and smoked with the GI's.
One day Minnie stepped on a mine
and they put all her parts
in a small plastic bag.
No one could find her pussy
for one last punch in the bush
but a few days later
Mickey is hit by a rocket
while smoking with the guys
and both his arms are blown off.
The medic tries to treat him
but the cigarette is still burning
in the fingers of the severed arm
and when it burns down to fingers
and burns them into charcoal
Mickey screams that he can
feel the burn and the medic
shoots home the morphine
and now the grunts
have to shine their own boots
and go in the bush
with five finger Mary.

TEA GARDEN GIRLS

The Tea Garden girls
dress to show
in an oriental way.
Skinny, with long black hair
to the small of their backs,
large oval eyes, small breasts,
very tight traditional dresses
slit almost to the waist.

Suzie sits next to me,
places her hand very lightly
on my leg just below my crotch.
When she leans to whisper in my ear
"Buy me some tea, GI?"
her breast presses into my arm
and her hand slides to my balls.
She is very pretty,
the prettiest thing
I've seen in months and months.
Silent, she moves my hand
under her dress to her thigh
and asks again.
She is the prettiest thing in the world,
I'm ready to burst through my pants,
but I say "No. No tea today, Suzie."
She is not so pretty when she's leaving.

CHILD BEGGAR

Rick is in some ville, somewhere in a green war
and maybe it's Ben Het and maybe not
but the guys are pumping the whores
and getting high on green beer and ripe grass—
SOP, search and get fucked.

It's a little cess pool of squalor,
dust and poverty, fear and starvation,
just a roadside hamlet on the road to hell.

The Mama-san is dressed in rags
and the kid is dressed in less.
She steps in front of Rick,
who is heading down the road,
and she picks up the kid's
hand to beg for food or a few piasters.

At the age of five the world
has not yet brought the kid to his knees
and he will not keep his hand,
palm up in the begging position.

As Rick begins to walk on by
Mama-san beats the kid on the head,
just a few good whacks to let him know
that times are tough and mom is boss.
She shoves him at Rick like
a stumbling drunk, but he won't
raise his hand palm up,
just stands staring down at the dirt
waiting for the next whack
and when it comes he lets out a yell
because Mama-san is through with the love taps
and is getting into serious education.
She jerks his hand, palm up,
into Ricks midsection
but the kid is crying now
and won't look at Rick
and Rick can't look at the kid.

He decides to side with the kid
and walks on by without rewarding
Mama-san's lesson and the beating
doesn't turn a profit.
The beating is Mama-san's gift to the kid.
Refusing to pay is Rick's gift to them both.
The kid's tears are his gift to the world.

The kid won't live out the year.

REVOLUTIONARIES IN NAM

Nixon, Sanderson and I
argue radical politics
in the Armory,
a Black, a Jew and a White boy.
We debate the merits of violence
as a tool for social change,
read aloud from *Soul On Ice*,
compare Huey Newton with Jesus Christ.

Sanderson rolls us joints,
gets pissed when I mis-quote Marx
"Dope is the opiate of the masses."
All whites are racists,
all men are sexists,
non-violence is inaction,
power is in the hands of the monied.

We're impressed by our conclusions
and totally unaware of their irony,
sitting in a U.S. Armory
in the middle of Vietnam.

MICHAEL ANDREWS

BOQ1

Flo has on her mini skirt tonight
and it covers nothing from ankle to crotch
so I know what I want for dinner
and I know I'm not going to get it.
Instead we are off for BOQ1 to tease the lifers
with round eye pussy and long legs
and to get some down home American dinner,
a filet mignon with a strip of fat soaked bacon
wrapped all around it and bayonetted with toothpicks,
a baked potato and a bowl of mystery soup.

Flo gets a case of modesty
and puts on the pants that
go under the mini skirt so
no swinging dick will get cheap thrills tonight.
My hair is way beyond regulation
and it gives the lifer sergeant
a serious case of ulcerated gas
and he wants me to get it cut
before he'll let me in his door
so I have pull rank on him—
what the hell, I'm a chicken shit colonel
in this chicken shit outfit
and if there is anything that an idiot
in green respects it's a bigger idiot in green
but he also doesn't like the pants on Flo
since ladies aren't regulation in pants
so she bends over and pulls them off
right there in front god and the brass
leaving nothing but legs
and a barely covered ass
so he has to let us through his door.

It's a BOQ so there are bachelors
and where there are bachelors there are waitresses
in very mini skirts and a no nonsense
attitude because they are making
top dollar without having to cohabit
with the enemy, just the occasional
wink and a goose which earns a bigger tip,
but they all look like they supplement their day job,
like they work the night life now and then
so they leave traces of perfume
and raw sex wafting through the air
but the steak is rare and greasy

and while I work on the baked potato
I get busy with the inside of Flo's thigh
under the oversized and starched tablecloth.

By now I am getting hungry for desert
and Flo doesn't brush me off her thighs
but she draws the line at rubbing her pussy
so before I can't stand up without being obvious
I leave a tip and watch Flo's ass
wiggle toward the sergeant's door
and leave the lifers and the bachelors
to eat the chocolate pudding
and I give the sergeant a wink
when I put my hand on that tight
little butt going back out his door.

DAVID WIDUP

THE PICTURE SHOW

Standing in line to see a movie,
back on the main base after months in the field,
I'm talking with my buddies,
smoking dope and drinking warm beer.
We're in the middle of a long line snaking
around the ugly cinderblock movie house.
It's dusk and I notice him by accident
as I look to see who from my squadron
is on guard duty at the ajacent lot under constuction,
a pussy job, building a new PX on Bien Hoa,
hot showers every night and gook whores.
I'm looking to see who the lucky jerk is
that's guarding our construction area tonight
when I see him walking through the area unchallenged.
My first thought is
"why the fuck isn't the guard challenging this guy?"
He's walking towards me
and I see by his new fatigues and boots
that he's green - a long timer
with many months to go.
He's holding his M-16 wrong,
it's magazine loaded
and he's holding it at his side by the pistol grip
instead of strapped over his shoulder - barrel down.
Then I notice his eyes - vacant, crazy, lost
and his shoulders are stooped and he's stumbling,
not drunk, but unaware of where he is,
he's crazy already and he's got over 300 days to go.

COFFIN LUMBER

The Saigon cemetery is a busy place.
Most of the dead get there the hard way,
carried on foot in a cheap wooden box
and planted in the brown sludge
of tropical mud and monsoon rain.
The rich ride in on the fancy hearse
pulled by the prancing white horses.
It looks like a nobleman's carriage
leftover from the French Revolution.

The coffin makers need a lot of lumber.
Adults use more wood and take less skill.
But the tiny coffins are harder work
and there are more of them—
800 coffins a week for the children of Saigon.
No one counts the children anywhere else.
No one counts the children who have left
no one behind able to pay for the coffin.

The coffin maker has sad eyes and a hard mouth.
All his children were killed a long time ago.
They killed his wife and they killed his mother,
his father and his brothers.
He makes each coffin like a jewel box.
He does it to eat and he never cries.
He doesn't know why he eats,
there is no good reason to keep it up—
he'll never have another child
but he knows exactly why he never cries.

He would like to live long enough
to hear the reason, or any reason at all.
He would like to live long enough
to see the children take their revenge.

He dreams at night of sleeping under mud.
He eats his white rice, the dead vegies
and the number ten nouc mam
while the black evening rain
washes blood from the sky
and Agent Orange down the Delta.
The mud swallows children
and complains of indigestion.

The children sleep beneath the mud

MICHAEL ANDREWS

waiting for a dry season—
the patient seeds of human nightmares.
Not a flower and not a tree,
not a fruit and not a weed
will tap their hungry roots
into the savage dreams
of these empty hearts.

THE POET'S HEART

Think of me in jungle fatigues
sitting on the perimeter
during Tet 1969 -
the sky on fire
and the smell of burning flesh
full in the air.

Think of my soul,
lost and floating
like the scent of the newly dead
and those still dying,
think of the spear through it,
thick and wooden and honest.

Words, too, pierce
like a knife through meat,
penetrating, excising,
not as a sacrifice,
but searching, like the soldiers
and the home they longed for.

Think, too, of Hemmingway's gunshot mind,
bleeding in the Cuban rocking chair,
that reached out to touch
the poet's heart.
The poet's heart,
what the guns and lies
could not kill.

MICHAEL ANDREWS

CAO DAI TEMPLE
1969, THE NAM

Along the Long Binh Highway there is a temple.
It's as big and splashy as an uptown Baptist church
and we ride in just to see what the local color is.

She is at least ninety and she doesn't
do English. Why should she?
She couldn't make a dime in a tea bar,
the army can't draft her
and many gods are on her side.
She tours us around and show us the holy stuff.

There is a mural above the door.
It shows all their saints doing their
saintly bits. There is Moses
and Jesus and Buddha and Mohamed and Confucius—
the stench of gods is pretty rank in here.
The Cao Dai used to be one of the best
fighting machines in the land of Nam.
That's because they were believers.
Diem put them out of the fighting business.

Now they believe in free market enterprise
and they run the biggest opium and gun
running markets along the Laotian border—
a Sunday market for the heavy hitters.

I'd say they have covered
their bases,
their bets
and their asses.

Better safe than sorry.

MY MAMA-SAN

My Mama-San is short,
with dark skin covering
her broad, open face.
She is handsome,
perfect posture,
even, white teeth,
ever polite,
always smiling,
only her eyes show the pain,
her black oval eyes
radiating the hurt that
reaches beyond tears,
she doesn't cry anymore,
her tears would be an acid
burning the ground black.

My Mama-San calls me "Mr. David",
she knows I'm in charge of the armory,
and security for our Squadron,
and the first three times
she tells me the V.C. are coming tonight,
I don't say or do anything different.
The first two times we get rocket attacks
and the third time satchel charges and mortars.
I ask her why she tells me
and she says because she likes Mr. David,
doesn't want him to be hurt.

My Mama-San washes the clothes,
shines the boots,
makes up the cots,
cleans the barracks,
for me and twenty other
Red Horse enlisted men,
on the perimeter at Bien Hoa.
She comes early in the morning
while I'm still in the armory
or up in the tower on the Hill.
She leaves after dark,
after she wakes me up with coffee,
talking very fast Vietnamese to me
that we both know I don't understand.
For a long while, I wonder what she is saying,
and after several months I don't care anymore,
I pretend her smiling words,

spoken at machine gun speed,
are gentle greetings and news of the day,
like a old married couple would exchange
in front of the fire at night.

My Mama-San drinks with the other Mama-sans
in Morton's cube with a few other guys
on New Year's Eve.
They all go off to get more drinks
and she sits on my knee
straddling it and kisses me hard,
her tongue deep in my mouth.
Before I get fully hard,
she stands up,
hugs my head to her breast,
says "Good-bye Mr. David",
and is out the cube,
down the aisle,
her black pajamas moving
at double time speed.

My Mama-San never comes back.
We are told she was killed
by V.C. in an attack against her small village
just northwest of Bien Hoa.
I know better.
She didn't get killed by them,
or beat by them,
she joined them.
I know,
her eyes told me
on New Year's Eve -
there were tears in them,
and they didn't burn the ground.

My Mama-San launches
mortars and rockets
at me and my buddies.
I think of her when I'm sitting in the bunkers,
loud explosions rocking the ground,
some of the young guys shaking
at their helplessness,
the smell of rot and sweat strong
in the sandbag huts we sit in,
night after night.
I think of her then, late at night,
kissing me hard, tears on her cheeks,

and her pajamas moving double time
down the barracks aisle on New Year's Eve.

MICHAEL ANDREWS

CENTRAL MARKET AND THE WORM DOCTOR

I am shopping for mosquito netting and meat.
The netting I buy from a little old lady
and by counting fingers, writing numbers
and talking pigeon she agrees to sew it
into a canopy to cover my bed,
to keep away the mosquitoes
and the dreams and the night.

The meat hangs in the central market
like painted red penitents
kneeling at the doors of some heaven
no one will ever be good enough to enter.
The meat is swarming with flies
which they brush away when serious
money gets involved.
I buy a slab of mystery meat,
cheese from Europe and apples from Dalat.

Outside there is a medicine man—
the Pied Piper of Vietnam.
He has a small army of children
with or without nervous, shrieking moms,
squatting over yesterday's news
and he makes them drink the medicine
until they shit away runny turds
and all their intestinal worms.

I catch a cab and bicker over the fare
under the Prill Toothpaste billboard
and I think about my meat and the flies
and about taking the good doctor's medicine
and I hand the meat over to the driver as a tip
and have him drop me off at the Rex
for a sawdust and axle grease hamburger.

Better safe than sorry.

FLO AND THE CYCLO RIDE

We are riding through the neon hells of Saigon
and the black light hides the ruts and pot holes
and it hides the men in the shadows stroking
the shafts of their guns, tickling
the rifle's clitoral trigger,
hoping for an excuse for the bullet
that is singing in the chamber
for blood and the sense of well being
that comes from fulfillment of purpose.

We have eaten a tuna grill at La Dolce Vita
and we catch the first cyclo
heading away from downtown,
out Cong Ly to Cach Mang
and we ride on the front seat,
two human bumpers
looking for a crash
while the engine explodes
many hundreds of times a minute
just beneath our butts
and the driver honks and curses through the traffic,
another fish in a sea of people
and when someone shouts
we don't pay any attention
and the driver pretends not to hear
until they fire the rifle into the air
and mostly they never think that
what goes up must come down,
or they just don't give a shit,
but the driver does because the next one
sings for him and he pulls over to the curb.

The ARVN soldier wants to get a little graft
because he sees an American with a girl
with long, black hair and thinks
he isn't getting the pussy so maybe
he can collect a few hundred piasters
for a license to fuck,
or maybe just prove he is the man
with the gun and the power
and with nothing better to do
but wait until curfew
to shoot at dogs and rats.

They always think that Flo is Vietnamese at night.

MICHAEL ANDREWS

He wanders over and sees that he has wasted
a bullet for nothing and waves us on
and Flo gets mad because she gets scared
when they start banging off live rounds
just to get our attention.
And when she gets scared she gets mad
and she bolts her knees together
and they won't crack until tomorrow.

So the soldier wins after all.

The driver doesn't like it either
and he curses in Vietnamese all the way
to our villa, and he curses when
I pay him and he curses when I tip him
and he curses after I have closed the gate
and he drives away, down Hoang Dieu
to go home before curfew sets in
to see if any of his children
have lived through the day.

Flo strips down to panties
but it's no use my putting on the classical music
or coping a feel
hoping to redeem the night.

I dodge an airborn roach,
turn off the pathetic yellow lights,
listen to the purr of the air conditioner
and wonder into whose life
that wasted bullet fell.

ON THE PERIMETER

It's dark on the perimeter,
I stare out into the dark,
my gun and radio drape across my lap.
My guards talk about sounds and sights,
trip flares, argue about pops
are they gunshots or wood breaking under foot?
I think they make them up.

Stars seem brighter than flares,
though I know they aren't.
I smoke another joint
and watch as the mechanics
fine tune the engines
of their fighters.
Why am I growing hard
looking at the ass end of something getting hot?

I'm hungry,
haven't eaten for days.
To distract myself from my hungers,
I take a dog for the night on the east end,
it's dark and late.
The dog's name is Telstar.
I feel the pull of his chain in my hand
and wonder how he shows
someone outside our range,
does he point his paw, lean his head
or tug on the chain?
I smoke another joint.
I feel the chain in my hand,
cold and hard and still.
I drop my gun in the ditch and look at the sky.
I drop the leash.
Telstar doesn't move.
I sit in the dirt and hug the dog.
He sits and drops his head in my lap
and falls asleep.

MICHAEL ANDREWS

YOU CAN SEE BY MY OUTFIT THAT I AM A GRUNT

In country only two weeks
and Bill finds a GI in the bush
with his ears cut off
and his cock jammed down his throat.
He watches the mutilated body until the choppers come
and the rotten black smile
crawls with the rictus of pearly teeth
and the chuckle of the maggots
and the biggest fear is not dying—
the biggest fear is killing.

That is, until death taps Bill on the shoulder.

Until Bill imagines his own death
he can't imagine killing.
It makes a guy hesitate the first time he pulls the trigger.
And that moment stuffs many a New Guy into a plastic bag.

Bill needs to see his best buddy die.
He has to be as near to death as a razor is to his chin.
Then he understands that his own death is as real
as the mud in his toes, as the rot in his crotch.
Bill understands he wants to live.
He understands he has to kill to stay alive.

The first enemy a soldier kills is himself.

The sergeant is a short timer
with a heart turned as hard as last year's fruit cake
and a terminal case of the thousand yard stare.
He knows that Bill needs
to kill his humanity to stay above ground.
He has to eat his heart to get out alive.

And he does.

After that Bill goes home and the war begins.
He has to find a reason why he should be alive.

He finds it at the bottom
of a fifth of Johnny Walker

and begins to kill the last living thing he knows.

SANDY

Sanderson is on the Hill tonight.
I leave the Armory and
drive along the perimeter
in the jeep.
It's clear and quiet
in the middle of the night.
I watch the perimeter where
nothing moves.

On the Hill,
Sanderson is sitting on the floor of the Tower.
I'm an idiot to put him up here,
he's worthless.
Busted down to the bottom,
a Black Panther,
dope smoker,
big,
black,
angry.

I ask Sandy for some dope.
He asks me for a cigarette.
I give him three.
He twists out the tobacco
and sucks in the grass.
I light one,
put two in the plastic cigarette case
I keep in the thigh pocket
of my jungle fatigues.

"Sandy, why are you here, man,
this ain't your war."
He's still on the floor.
I'm now staring out the tower,
searching for light, motion.
The compound looks dark tonight,
darker than usual.
I notice one of the generator lights out.
"I came to learn how to kill White boys.
Now I'm just waiting to get thrown out and sent home."
He says the same thing
every time I ask.
I ask when the North generator went out.
Sandy's quiet,
I'm thinking he's asleep.

DAVID WIDUP

I lift the hatch in the center of the tower floor
to climb down the stairs.
Five steps down,
I reach up to close the cover
(wouldn't want Sandy to fall through)
and he says
"I sold the generator to Charlie.
Don't mean nothin."

THE GECKO AND THE BEANIE WEANIES

It is good luck to have geckos in the house.
They are green and fat and can walk
upside down across our ceilings.
They pop out of the most unexpected places,
crawl along the ceiling, knock out a few
upside down push-ups perilously close
to the whaping fan and stalk moths and roaches.

The roaches are the size of child's fist.
And these days we need all the luck we can get.
It takes a few months for Flo to get used to the
idea of green lizards crawling around her kitchen.
In the end she decides that they are pets.

One of them lives behind the stove.
Flo has taught him to sprint up the table
and whisk away bits of food that she leaves
like sacrificial offerings near the table edge.
He is not so crazy about stalking roaches now.
This evening I am sitting in peace, locked away
from the war, reading and writing and ignoring life.
I do not want to leave this couch, ever.
Flo is in the kitchen, bustling over beanie weenies.
This is a major treat for me, straight out of
the deli section of the commissary.
"Yum, yum," I think, "beanie weenies."

"Michael. Come here, watch this gecko."
No response comes to mind, so I ignore it.
No way am I moving off this couch for a gecko.
A few pages go by. "Michael," she yells,
excited as a kid watching kittens being born,
"he eats beanie weenies."
"Less for me," I think, turning the page.
Finally she runs into the living room bouncing
and jiggling in her underwear, and for a moment
the idea of the bed sounds better than the couch,
but she blathers on about this magic gecko.
"He's eaten seven beanie weenies," pulling me
by the arm, "come and watch. So cute."

So much for peace, or even a sweaty toss in the sheets.
Who cares about some gluttonous gecko.
"Geckos," I pontificate, "do not eat beanie weenies.
Besides, seven of them would pop his stomach."

MICHAEL ANDREWS

So here I am, standing in the kitchen, a solemn witness
to a hitherto unknown event in the behavior of geckos.
Flo puts a single beanie weenie, sopping with
sugary tomato sauce on the edge of the table.
Sure enough, his head pops over the edge,
rotates left, then right, then twists clockwise,
counter-clockwise, looks up and then down,
then right at the beanie weenie, his tongue flicking
in and out and whipping around in
a frenzy of beanie weenie lust.

He suddenly leaps onto the table top,
grabs the beanie weenie in his jaws and jumps
over the edge, disappearing down the back.
"I don't believe it," I say.
Flo is triumphant. "I will feed him
beanie weenies every night."

A sudden sense of impending doom prompts me
to investigate this gecko scientifically.
It is either that or face a long
and serious beanie weenie shortage.
"If I let go of the beanie weenies today,"
I think, "tomorrow it will be the Oreo cookies."
I move the stove and look beneath the table.
I find seven naked beans and the gecko
licking the sauce from the eighth.

"You have addicted this poor innocent lizard
to junk food," I say, presenting her with the evidence.
I head back to the relative calm of the couch
while Flo scolds the gecko for tricking her.
She is not so pissed at the gecko
as she is at me for being right.

If I dare to chuckle she will throw
cans of beanie weenies at me all night long.
As it is, my sex life tonight is in jeopardy.
I keep my chuckles to myself and go back to my book.

The gecko goes back to roaches.

FLARES, TRUTH AND THE COLD BLACK GHOST

In the black, Saigon sky
the flares float like slow motion
stars, acetylene and phosphorus
painting the night with truth
about the earth below.

I had a heart then, just like yours
and just like yours, it thought
the world was a picture of the sun
reflecting in a puddle
left by the afternoon rain.

On the morning patrol
the Bouncing Betty
leaps into the air
like an insane Jack in the Box
springing up from Pop Goes the Weasel,
traumatically amputates Pierce's left leg
and leaves the right a shredded beef Hero sandwich.

He screams until the morphine
brings peace to the jungle birds,
asks Doc about his balls
and falls into an ice-cold shock.

They radio for a dust off
and set off the smoke to guide the pilot
when an AK-47 punches holes in Sanchez
like a Singer sewing machine stitches a hem
and the Medivac veers away
and even though Sanchez could die
from the sucking chest wound
sergeant Dunne thinks about how
he hates the little prick when he
mooches someone else's fruit cocktail.

Co Trang's tunnel entrance is big enough for her,
but a tight squeeze for the overfed American's.
She sits in the black cool of the tunnel,
shaking with the fear and adrenalin.
She is waiting around the second bend
for what she guesses must come next.
She plugs wax and cotton in her ears
to muffle the concussion of the grenades.
Her family is a cold, black ghost.

Her father was killed by hungry ARVN
pillaging the farm for chickens.
Her brothers were killed by napalm and bad luck.
Her mother starved to death in a relocation
camp and didn't seem to mind.
The frozen, black ghost lives in her bowels,
which are loose and watery and angry.
It is turning her heart into shiny, black plastic.
The VC gave her food, weapons and a purpose.
She knows the frozen, black ghost
wants to eat many, many hearts
and she knows she can pass it on to others
just like a curse, a cold or a case of dysentery.
She wants to plant the ghost
in the hearts of big, pasty colored Americans.

In the green flaming jungles north of Saigon
a six year old girl reaches up and touches my face
like a flare penetrating a black sky and in the deep,
brown pools of her eyes, she saves my life.

I am sure her heart has never turned black and frozen.
I am sure that we have both kept the promise
made by my face and her small, brown hand,
that our hearts will always pump blood,
that our hands make only love,
that our tears keep the memory.

By lot sergeant Dunne sends Hayes into the tunnel.
It is a relief not to send his best friend, Wilson,
and Hayes is as smart and experienced as
an eighteen year old virgin can be.
He lowers himself into the entrance
and where his toes just reach the floor
his chest gets wedged and Co Trang drives
her knife up into his balls and penis,
deep into his bowels, while Hayes kicks and screams.
She twists the blade and levers it from front to back
and scrambles away from his thrashing legs.
She leaves the knife because she knows
that with it goes a little bit of the black ghost
and she scrambles back into the safety of the tunnel.

Sergeant Dunne holds Hayes down while Doc
pulls out the knife and Hayes passes into
that tiny paradise where pain takes us
when the world finally tells the truth.

Sanchez and Pierce are dead, but the dust off
takes Hayes away where a doctor
with a frozen, black heart will save his life
to spend wondering how things might have been
if only he could get an erection.

By noon it is over a hundred degrees
when they flush Co Trang from the tunnel,
bleeding from her ears and already
deep into her death trance.

Hayes has a buddy named Pritchard
who is dumb, loyal and way beyond crazy.
He beats Trang for a while, then spreads her legs
and rapes away his fear and joy and the last
shreds of his sanity, and two more
follow Pritchard while Co Trang
dreams of her family and of passing on
the hungry, black ghost.

Sergeant Dunne loses his erection when she
doesn't scream or fight or even pay attention.
His eyes fix forever at a thousand yards
and his mind seizes up in rust and sludge,
clanks to a stop and his eyes go blind
with the red and green flames that burn
the earth black and blue and dead, dead, dead.
He puts his flare gun into Co Trang's pussy,
jerks her hair so he can look into her eyes
and the moment that he pulls the trigger
his dreams will swear forever that she smiles.

Sergeant Dunne does not pause to consider
what brings him the joy—the pain,
the love, the hate or the cold, black indifference.
The frozen, black ghost settles into his
lower intestines and reaches up to squeeze
his heart in its strong, black fist.
Sergeant Dunne does not believe that he is going
to live through the day, and
sergeant Dunne does not give a rusty fuck.

Waiting for the traffic to cross Nguyen Hue
a hard faced whore in a blood red miniskirt
puts her hand on my ass and whispers hot,
wet words in my ear, "Fuck you, suck you
numbah one. Ten dollah MPC,"

and her smile almost takes the edge off her eyes
while my prick leaps to attention.
It's the nicest thing someone has said to me
all day long, but I cross the street instead,
looking for a place the change my money.

I shoot this poem into the ice black sky
trying to paint the truth about the earth below.
There are things about war that you don't want to know.
We know that the frozen, black ghost stalks us
in the night, waits in the shadows of a back alley.
We can pass on the disease,
but we can't pass the cure.

This poem can not transmit the truth of it.
And even if it could—

you could never get it.

THE BLACK TIGER

At night on the perimeter near Tuy Hoa,
    the black tiger comes to visit when the moon
    is new and the wet sky is thick and black
    the stars pinholes in a blanket covering the light.

The tiger watches me from beyond the third fence,
    without a scope I can only see his eyes and the outline
    of his head, emeralds moving in space just above the
    ground that stare at me with the knowledge of centuries.

He moves slowly, keeping his stare on me,
    he moves sideways, from right to left,
    and left to right, only occasionally
    looking down to see where he is going.

After weeks of nightly visits, the black tiger
    finally gets its own, stepping on a land mine
    the explosion moving the ground like a morter, and
    I swear I saw him fly right through that blanket in the sky.

MICHAEL ANDREWS

HOME LEAVE

We pack our terror in the cupboard
so we can find it when we get back.
We swim through the humidity to the airport
and settle into the refrigerated 707.
18 hours later we are strolling
down Westwood Boulevard, milling
with a crowd of mindless shoppers.
They seem to be mostly interested in
color coordinating their socks,
getting more money, more perqs,
more status, more things, more ahead,
buying the latest Simon & Garfunkle
and knowing where the best spaghetti is.

We go to see a movie—Catch 22.
The theater is air conditioned
so I have to wear a sweater.
I sit on the aisle where we have
a clear shot to a clean get-away.

The movie is all about war and insanity.
Naturally the terms are synonymous
but these people don't seem to know that.
All kinds of crazy shit is going on
and I fidget in my seat, jump at the
fight scenes, get a little crazy myself
thinking, "Yeah, this is it.
This is Saigon—it's the Republic, this
is what is happening; corruption,
mindless futility, terror, insanity.

When the lights go up I'm exhausted,
worried I can't get to an exit
before someone rockets the theater.
I expect to see an audience transformed,
shocked into sudden realization,
to stunned to move knowing now what
war is all about and determined
to march out of this theater
and put a complete and total stop to it.

Instead they yawn, shuffle to their feet
and herd along toward the exits
chatting about red socks and blue shoes.

"Shit," I hear from somewhere
in the bowels of the audience,
"crap like that never happens."

I sit tight in my chair
until the crowd flushes out to Westwood.
I am sweating and freezing
and grinding my teeth while I am awake.

"Got to get back to Nam," I mutter.
"Got to get back where the madness is real.
Can't stay here where the madness
is nothing more than entertainment for idiots."

I am digesting this whole new
picture of the concept of sanity
when this local citizen rams
a fist full of popcorn into his grin,
glances my way and says, "Fuck war.
Say, what about them Dodgers, huh?"
I lunge over theater seats and pod people.
I am going to see if his smile improves
while I shove that hot buttered popcorn
up his rosy red rectum, kernel
by fucking
kernel.

The credits roll to a stop.
The lights go up.
The humans fade like ghosts.
They have lost solidity.
They have become transparent cartoons
flitting about this Disneyworld called home.

Home dies forever in a theater in Westwood.

We stagger out to the streets
that I used to have names for.
I am completely lost.
I am a confused foreigner
in an alien city without a map,
without a dictionary.
I am more afraid of them than
being lost in a blood and green jungle.
I feel for my weapon.
I find a shopping bag and camera.
I watch the non-people.

MICHAEL ANDREWS

I don't know who the enemy is.

I begin counting down
the five days back to Nam.
I will never again be able to consider
the Homo Americanus as
a seriously real being.

Catch 22 received no awards.

DAVID WIDUP

A STOLEN MOMENT

Once, I stole a moment from death,
not knowing it would be taken back
one hundred, no one thousand fold.
I stole it for Sam, dressed in jungle fatigues,
his legs coved in the blood that ran like rivers of pain,
streams of ending life from wounds in his belly
that now held as much metal shrapnel as life.
The path we sat on was worn down
by the marches of death that had gone on
for centuries, endless lines of tired men
walking with weapons through the thick humid air
from the jungles across the small rice paddies.

We sat in the small gutter in the center of the path,
I held his shoulders in my arms
the way I now hold my teenage boys,
too big for me to hug but too needy for me to leave alone.
My arms ached and quivered as flashes and sulphur
filled the early morning air.
Sam felt no pain, but was very thirsty,
he emptied his small canteen
and was working his way through mine
when the blood first started falling
from the corner of his mouth, first just one small drop
so I thought maybe he had just cut his lip.
But no, no he was dying and I knew it
when the drops came too close together,
they filled the space in time between one another
and formed a thin red line down his chin.
He couldn't remember my name,
kept calling me Tom, and his name, Sam,
looking backward over his head,
as if there were something worse
than dying in a Vietnam jungle
at the beginning of the day.
He kept licking his lips with his dry tongue,
they were chapped and cracking.
I wondered if they would open up and bleed too.
He looked through me and called me Sam,
Sam help me stand up,
I want to stand up just one more time.
I took off my fatigue jacket and made tourniquets
to stop the blood from coming out of the slashes
in his thighs and wrapped the rest around his stomach,
open for all the world to see

DAVID WIDUP

like he was on an Operating Room table
or maybe being made by God in the morning mist.
I grabbed him from behind and lifted him
by unbending my knees,
him leaning into me like the weight of life.
He was barely up and staring at the horizon facing us
before his last breath went out, slow and very, very long
and he seemed a little lighter
once there was no life left in him,
and he collapsed like a bag of meat at my feet.
There was nothing left of Sam for me,
nothing at all alive at my feet.

Last night, I was alone and sick
and my dreams come in short waves
like the angry ocean into a narrow bay.
In them, I'm Sam.
There is no one to pick me up,
no one to lift my eyes to the green edge of the earth,
no one to hold me as my life goes away slowly,
my sight going narrow, blurry and then gone.
No one to feel me as I go away one last time.
I die alone in the war path gutter.
My blood filling it for no one.

CO TRINH WATCHES FROM THE TREES

Co Trinh watches him from the tree
sweating over her body
like a water buffalo
stuck in the mud.

He surprised her after they burned the village.
She was hiding in the forest
out of her mind with the fear
that her mother or her sister had been killed
and when he came crashing through the brush
shooting insanely at an escaping pig
she couldn't keep the whimper
from exploding from her throat
and he jumped on top of her
smashing her into the ground
with that immense weight
and she saw the light in his eyes
flicker from insanity to rape
and she began to scream when he tore
away her pants, but his fist
crashed into her temple so hard
that she could not move and the limbs
of the trees swirled like a kaleidoscope
against the sky and when his raging
cock tore into her private thoughts
she suddenly found herself sitting—
high in this tree watching him
buck and thrust against her body,
scraped and jerked along the ground.

They are so far and so far away
that they might as well be two
strangers fucking in the forest.
The dance of the clouds in the sky
seems more important at the moment,
but she remembers whose body it is
bearing that immense rage of weight
and she looks down just as
he flexes rigid as a gutted pig
and with a small groan collapses
like a snake along a limb.
He sits up on his knees
arranging his pants with his clumsy hands
and reaches for his rifle
and for a moment Co Trinh can see

MICHAEL ANDREWS

the murder that crosses his eyes
before he notices that she is unconscious
or perhaps already dead
and then she sees the thing in his eyes
that makes it possible for her to live
a long, long time — the sudden realization
of all the nightmares that will hunt
him in his dreams, the guilt he will
never acknowledge eating holes
in his belly, the women who will never
know about this moment in a jungle
but who will know anyway
and leave him with his raging penis
and his broken heart.

When her body calls her back
she doesn't want the pain.
She remembers that she has to find her mother.

She tells herself that
if she has a child she will kill it.
But if she cannot kill it, she knows she will not love it.
And even if she does love it,
she will teach it to hate the Americans.
If it is a girl she will teach her to hate men.

If it is a boy,
she will teach him
to hate himself.

FLO'S PEE AND THE NEARLY DEAD

She has to have a urine test to make a happy doctor.
The happy doctor will cheerfully take our money
and give Flo a piece of paper
that will turn into birth control pills.
And controlling birth
is high on our priorities.

She's in her miniskirt, looking good,
legs and ass and long dark hair
and the Lt. Doctor says "Fill this up,"
and hands her the glass jar.
It isn't dark glass, it's see through glass.
We have to ask where she does this
and it turns out to be through half the wards
filled up with the half-alive and the nearly dead
who were lucky enough to survive
some mind crushing brush with death
and now they are merely mutilated
but most of them have eyes and nothing
better to do but keep them open
for passing nurses, donut dollies
and any kind of round eye pussy.

"What will I do," she frets,
"they're all going to see me carrying
my pee in this little glass jar."

"The only thing you can do," I offer
with the only solution that comes to mind,
"is hold your pee high and walk tall."

And so she does.
I know when she is coming back
by the cat calls and whistles
and she looks flushed but proud
and I think we did the boys a favor
but after we get our piece of paper
and turn it into pills
I rush her back to the villa
in the skimpy skirt
to give them pills

the acid test.

MICHAEL ANDREWS

THE FREEZING SWEATS

I bust out of the quonset's
refrigerated cigarette smoke
into the rotting steam of the Nam
and I run around Ton Son Nhut
toward the backside where there is
always smoke from burning
tires and the military junk.
They burn the mutilated armor
and the shot-up airplanes
and sooner or later I run
by the morgue
where they bring the junked boys
after the choppers dump them
at Third Field Hospital
like skids of hot dogs
heading for the weenie roast.

They come in their body bags—
the last new suit the Army gives them.
A body bag is a sack of dreams
on the way to the ovens.
No one here is almost dead.
No one here is almost pregnant.

It is a parking lot of boxes
shining silver and blazing
aluminum, stacked in the sun
like Vietnamese condominiums
waiting for their tenants.

In the end the dreams were simple—
going home, a girl to tickle,
a decent cheeseburger and
living through the day.

Boxes of dreams on their way home.

Someone in the world will
put these dreams in the ground,
throw over the dirt, drip
the tears and plant the daisies.

I keep on running
just for the cheap thrill
of feeling the air pump in
and the air pump out.
The sweat freezes to my skin.
I am alive in the Nam—

and even my nightmares
are trivial.

DAVID WIDUP

THE EGRET

The large egret flies slowly, wings out
        and barely moving over the rice fields
        green with life and swollen buds -
        a fertile field ready to be harvested.

The bird circles the field in a lazy
        haphazard way, seeming to wander.
        The air is moist, thick and quiet
        only the egret is moving.

The rice fields are in squares, bounded
        by raised mud paths on all four sides.
        The water in the fields is so high
        that it almost spills over the path.

Neither the egret nor the rice knows of
        the blood that has washed into them for decades,
        of the mines in the adjacent jungle or the
        dead bodies rotting in the water in the corner field.

THE XTIAN MONTAGNARD

1
"They are such animals," Dung scowls,
like she had bitten off a mouthful of rotten mango,
"they are like wild pigs."
Dung has a college degree from the University in Dalat.
She thinks that the Montagnards are superstitious.
"Moi," she calls them, savages, and shudders.

Dung is afraid of ghosts in the night
and she believes that communists are evil.
Dung is a good Catholic girl.

She works with us in the slums of MACV
as a technical artist, drawing little boxes
and charts simple enough even for an ambassador to read.
The boxes and charts prove that we are winning the war,
counting up the bodies and totaling up the hamlets,
tracking the fluctuating curve of kill ratios
and the Commissaries supply of beanie-weanies.

Dung has a sister that is holier than all of us together.
Sanh is a nun. She undergoes fantastic hardships in the mountains
where she is busy trying to convert the animals into Christians.

"Not so easy, making Christians out of Moi," Dung tells us.

2
Doug Hardy tells me all about the Yards.
He lived with them as a Green Beret.
He says they're honest, work hard, don't steal and laugh a lot.
The Yards think like the Americans think—
it's the Vietnamese that are lazy, who lie, cheat and steal.
The Yards call the Vietnamese Yuan.

Everyone agrees.

3
Sanh leaves Ban Me Thuot, which is near Dalat,
in the mountains that are trying to reach heaven,
climbing out of death and insanity toward the clouds.
On foot she travels many days to Dien Kric.
It is the farthest as far can get, past the Da Mrong valley,
surrounded by green peaks that tickle the passing clouds.

Sanh does not get the beauty of it.
She is disgusted with the filth and the bad manners.
There are no cabs, no croissants, no telephones—
just pigs and people living in the dirt
eating grasshoppers and fermented rice.

She is preaching to the Moi about brotherly love,
about Jesus and salvation, heaven
and a major dose of hell.
Hell is something that Yards have a firsthand knowledge of.

They worship trees and stones and babbling brooks.
Every child knows the danger of offending the spirits.
They pour libations to appease the troubled spirits.
The children are busy trapping fish in the mountain streams,
catching grasshoppers for a snack
and chasing the birds away from the grain.

Hell doesn't mean a thing to them.

4

But one man does listen. His name is Ja Had
and Ja Had is a serious man.
Ja Had thinks that when any person speaks
he has something true to say.
It is a big idea, a single spirit
that lives in everything at once.
Y Blar the sorcerer has always told them
that they are born again and again,
sometimes in the rat, sometimes in the tree.
If we eat the pig, the pig may be born as our child.

It is a great sin to waste food.
If we leave a place, we must carry all the food.
The food we cannot carry, we must eat.
The animal's spirit would be angered with waste.
To die for nothing is offensive even
to a spirit that lives in everything.

"Tell me more about this big spirit,"
Ja Had asks of Sanh.
Sanh is worn out trying to explain Sin and Heaven
to the savages. They can't grasp the simplest truth.
But she is eager to explain it Ja Had
who listens with two ears and asks many questions.
They eat grain mush and river fish
sitting under the trees, as the mountains

tickle the clouds, and the clouds
drench the fields.

"If you die without Baptism, you will go to the evil place.
You will not be born again.
You will go there forever.
If you take the water ceremony, the big spirit
will take you to his house above the clouds.
You will never be hungry, you will laugh all day long."

"I am confused," admits Ja Had.
"Y Blar the sorcerer is very wise.
He tells us a different truth.
I must consider if it is possible for both truths to be true."

In Ja Had's house Sanh is talking with K'Brung.
K'Brung is Ja Had's wife for many years.
She asks if the big spirit can give them children.
Sahn is sure that the reason they cannot have children
is because they have already committed some great sin
and they have offended God, the big spirit.
Ja Had is making her listen to Sanh's words.
When K'Tueh returns from the fields
Sanh asks if this is their daughter.
"This is K'Tueh, my second wife," Ja Had says.

For an hour Sanh tries to hammer into them
that to be a Christian Ja Had can only have one wife.
This is not a thing that is easy to understand.
"Why does the big spirit care how many wives I have?
Most of the men have more than one wife."

"They will go to the evil place forever," states Sanh.
"I will return in one month to hear your answer."

Sanh is glad to think she may have a convert.
If she can get one, then she can get others.
If she gets many, the Bishop will be pleased.
She is thinking of hot baths and real food.

She returns to the nunnery and later she tells
her sister Dung all about her Christian Montagnard.

    5
Dung pulls the live snail from the pale of water.
She spears it with a small fork and twists it out.
She wraps it in sticky rice and nouc mam

and chews it slowly as she considers her words.
She is telling us about her sister the nun
and her sister's Christian Montagnard.
Perhaps the Moi can learn to be civilized after all.

6
When Ja Had married K'Tueh as his second wife
the heavy gongs bonged across the valley
and the kamboat mouth pipe warbled
like a forest of birds singing in the dawn
and they drank the burning rice wine while Y Blar
performed the ceremony where they exchanged
the brass wire bracelets and then they drank
the fermented honey, sweet and fiery
and filled with many juicy flies and crunchy ants.

It was Ja Had and K'Brung's hope
that K'Tueh would deliver them the child
that the spirits had held from them
even though they poured rice wine daily
at the stone in which the spirit lived
that guarded their house.

Tonight they sit weeping and talking.
For two days they talked with Y Blar.
He tells them of the spirit in the tree
that could make a child for them.
K'Brung thought that would be enough,
let the Yuan keep their big spirit and his evil place.
And after they died, they would have many children
to pour rice wine for their thirsty spirits.

But K'Tueh thought otherwise,
that a place to live forever and be happy
was a very big idea, and all Ja Had must do
is take the water ceremony and have only one wife.
They would still have children to make their spirits happy.
It was only fitting because of their love
for one another that Ja Had should find a place
in the big spirit's house for all of them.

But Ja Had could not give K'Tueh back to her mother.
It would be a great shame, and no man would take her.
She would starve and could not take part in the ceremonies,
her spirit would haunt the entire tribe for many generations,
make them tired, make them sick and bring bad luck.

MICHAEL ANDREWS

No, Ja Had could not do that to K'Tueh
even for the big spirit's happy place
and K'Brung said no, refusing to consider such a cruel thing
not for an entire tribe of children,
not even to stay out of the big spirit's evil place.

That night Ja Had made tender love to K'Tueh.
When they finished she fell asleep between
Ja Had and K'Brung as they wept
soft and steady like
the afternoon rains,
when the birds do not sing
and you cannot see the sky.

K'Tueh had told them what must be done.

    7
Sanh left the quiet peace of her bed
and the sweet ritual of tea and croissants in the afternoon
and made the journey by foot with greater hope than before,
up and over the high and hard mountain paths.

She allows herself to be eager to see if the seeds
she had planted a month earlier in the hard ground
of Dien Kric had sprouted any converts.
She thinks of Ja Had and his filed teeth
watching the rain beneath the giant mahogany tree,
weighing the threat of hell and the promise of salvation
against his small, young wife and her wide, fertile hips.
They are animals, she thinks, he has no idea of salvation.

That evening she arrives late in the village,
but Ja Had takes her directly to his bamboo and thatch house
sitting high above the squealing pigs on stilts.
Ja Had smokes his sweet mountain tobacco that he has
grown in last year's buffalo pen.
The village throbs with the slow and monotonous repeating
of the simple music of the gongs and the kamboat.
The rain falls as steady and quiet as the tears
of the homeless spirits, who wander without
ancestors to leave them bits of fish and a taste of rice wine.
K'Brung sips the rice wine first.
It is her very best, over a month fermenting in the jar.
She passes the wine to Sanh, who sips
the heat greatfully and passes it on to Ja Had.

Ja Had says, "I am a Christian now.

I am ready for the water ceremony."

"Wonderful," exclaims Sanh, "I am sure
that the Great God will be very happy."

"Will the big spirit give us children?" ask K'Brung.

"I'm sure he will bless you with many children
if you are good Christians," Sanh assures them.
"But how did you provide for your other wife?
Did you find her another husband,
or did you return her to her parents?"

"We did as K'Tueh instructed us.
We talked many days with Y'Blar the sorcerer.
He gave us a medicine for K'Tueh
and when she had died in the ceremony, we ate her."

"You killed her?" Sanh screamed
making herself choke on the fiery rice wine,
"and then you ate her like a young dog?"

"There was no choice," said K'Brung.
"There was no place for her to go
and so she would have died alone and in pain.
This way she died with a purpose.
She died with no pain and with those she loved.
She will be a happy spirit.
And when the big spirit blesses us
she will return to us as our child.
It was the only path that made us all happy.
I miss talking with her in the afternoon rain.
I am eager for her to come to us again."

"When can I take the water ceremony," Ja Had asks?

"You will never have Baptism," Sanh hisses
staggering to door, "you are savages, animals.
God could never love such beasts."
Sanh goes out into night, into the steady
fall of the rain and the endless throb of the gongs
and Ja Had and K'Brung weep all night
in the terror and the sorrow
of a spirit without a home.

8

The following week the sorcerer Y'Blar
makes them a ceremony to ease their spirits
and to appease the spirit of K'Tueh.
He gives K'Brung the medicine made from
the tree of the spirit that brings children.
Every afternoon Ja Had sits beneath the mahogany tree.
He listens to the rain, and sometimes to the birds.
He never plays the kamboat flute.

In the spring a small girl comes to K'Brung.

The name they give her is K'Tueh.

9

Sanh returns to the afternoon teas and buttered croissants.
She tells the Bishop of her failure
and the Bishop sends her out again.
She has become a relentless convertor of the Moi,
but she never goes to the village of Dien Kric,
circled by the high green mountains
and the ticklish afternoon clouds.

She tells her sister, Dung, all about
the savage that ate his wife.

She prays every afternoon for the salvation of their souls.
For pennance she gives up sweet tea and croissants.

10

Always in the afternoon, after eating
the eggs with the tiny embryos, the tiny
crunchy bones and the immature feathers,
the Vietnamese ladies sleep
away the heat and the war
and the attentions of the American men,
who are crude and aggressive
and sometimes mean.

Dung tells us all about her sister Sanh the nun
and about Ja Had the Christian Montagnard.

"They are animals," she states and then sighs,
"but my sister says they are just children and that
they have souls and she tries her best to save them."

MICHAEL ANDREWS

11
This poem is for the spirits of Ja Had the Christian Mantagnard,
for his wife, K'Brung, who makes the best rice wine
and for their child, K'Tueh
who keeps the birds from the rice
and sits with her father under the mahogany tree
playing the kamboat like a forest of birds—
for the high green mountains,
for the ticklish clouds

and for the afternoon rain.

STARING AT THE MAP

For hours and hours,
I sit in the Armory,
all night long,
with three radios,
coffee,
Winstons,
and a map of Vietnam.

Sometimes,
the base radio will call out
"Da Nang, under attack"
or
"Phan Rang under attack"
or
"Hue under attack"
or
"Bien Hoa under attack".
I look up at the map of Vietnam
on the wall in front of me
and find the base under attack
before writing in the Log Book
the time and place
in red ink.

In twelve months,
I memorize the map,
thinking of my friends in bunkers,
in field hospitals, dying,
with only incompetent Medics
and fellow wounded
to care for them.
I know the places
and the dates and times.
I think I'm fortunate
to still be breathing.
I listen to too many friends dying
on the radio in the Armory,
staring at a map of Vietnam.
And slowly,
the map takes my soul away.

CHOPPERS

Steel dragonflies joust above the Delta,
back and forth over this swamp of human dreams—
Vietnam sweats in the monsoon afternoon.
The choppers beat the air, claps of thunder,
palms slapping the underbelly of the sky
like air born medicine men
calling for rain.

All night they hover above Saigon,
criss-crossing the black agony
of the unknown, artfully
dodging the occasional flares
that sprout like the dreams of tiny suns
to wash away the dark,
the nightmares
and the fear.

They make the noise
that brings rescue and the fear
in the night,
in my dreams,
and in the waking nightmares
of the broad daylight
they take on the markings of red crosses
and deliver the human
chunks of GI meat
to the ER at Third Field
and to Grave's Registration
at the Ton Son Nhut Morgue.

When a chopper finally dies
it is recycled
into fragmentation grenades
and aluminum caskets.

They come sudden
whacking at the air
and they always bring
popsicle chills down my spine
in the broiling heat of war
and whether it is killing
or if it is saving
a chopper just beats the fun
right out of the sky.

MICHAEL ANDREWS

THE TIGER CAGES OF CON SON ISLAND

"If you are innocent, we will beat you until you are guilty."
The Ho Chi Minh University, Aug 1970

I didn't read about it in Stars and Stripes.
It came to me in Newsweek and Ramparts.
It is August now, and hot and I can walk
in the evening sweat while puss drips from the sky.

In 1861 the French Legionaires built the prison
on Con Son Island when the Emperor abdicated
three provinces adjacent to Saigon.
Now the US citizen pays taxes to two countries.
First in line to get paid is the US of A.
But 90% of South Vietnam's expenditures
are also paid by fun loving US citizens.
And this is what that tax dollar buys—
the Tiger Cages were built by USAID,
five feet by nine stone pits with bars above
and two to five men in a cage,
or five women, ages fifteen to seventy
with deep pink eyes filled with puss,
stove open skulls
and missing fingers.
They lose the fingers learning lessons.

I'm a slow learner myself.
I read about it and my eyes
do not fill with puss,
they fill with tears and the tears
are clean, pure and as useless
as a free fire zone.

The lesson is this:
don't get arrested in the Republic.
You end up on Con Son Island
playing soccer with Colonel Nguyen Van Ve.

In April of 1970 students were put on display
in the Saigon College of Agriculture
like entrants in a 4H Club fair.
They were in shock and they got their
dinner through a tube in their arms.
They had bamboo up their fingernails
and they were deaf from having soapy water
poured in their ears and then pounded.

MICHAEL ANDREWS

The soapy water was also used to pour
down throats until the digestive tracts
were destroyed and now they just shit green soup.
The women were raped and tortured
by the first district police
for having drugs and false documents.

If you fail to salute the flag
when they bring you to Con Son
you go into the Tiger Cages,
through a tiny, locked door
into the bowels of the earth
where you can't be seen,
where you can't be heard,
where your name is burried under
the stink of your own excrement.
Nguyen Minh Chau runs the Tiger Cages.
They call him "The Reformer."

I drive home in the sweating dusk,
take my shower and wash away the news.
No one seems to mind here,
no one seems to notice.
The prisoners don't get showers.
They get dowsed with lime and water
until it boils off their hair and skin.
When the lime rains down from the guards above
they can't breath from all the
blood coughing up with the lime.

The guards, members of the same species,
representatives of homo sapiens,
powder the prisoners with lime
and then they piss on them—
but only if they have to go.
Pissing on the prisoners is not mandatory,
just recommended procedure.

If they ask for vegetables they get rotten fish.
Gourmet rice is served filled with sand and pebbles.
You live in stone and you eat the stone.
In time, you turn into stone.
In time, stone is all that's left.

No more trouble buying shoes.
Tiger Cage people can't walk.
The trick is to bolt the legs to the stone floor,

MICHAEL ANDREWS

chains and shackles and the shackles
eat the skin, eat the muscle, eat the bone
until the legs atrophy to pale stone,
whithered pillars with coarse bark for skin,
human crabs scuttling along the pavement.
The lucky ones have wheels and wooden pallets.

I can walk.
I can pay my taxes and when I breath
not a drop of blood exhales.
In the afternoon furnace I run
around MACV on two strong legs—
and legs are not forever.
For lunch I want to get laid
but I have to settle for
strawberry ice cream from Givrals.

"Once I was a tailor," said Anh Ba.
"Maybe medicine and food
will make me walk again."
And if pigs could fly
we'd call them hummingbirds.

Once I was an analyst,
a technician of death.
I never laid a hand on a victim.
Victims are numbers in a machine.
Someone else arrests someone they don't like—
someone to extort a bribe from,
someone to get out of the way.
someone who has a job to get,
someone to tag as VCI on a Phoenix hit list,
someone to salt away on Con Son,
and five years later they rise from the ashes
of their own, burned out flesh.

When the prisoners are turned loose
they fly them to Saigon—
no legs, no money, no friends
and they dump them on a street corner
to crawl on their hands,
to drag their legs and beg until
they whither away,
so much stone
melting into stone.

After the shit hit the news fan

they moved the prisoners out of the Tiger Cages
and into the Cow Cages. The Cow Cages
were worse, barbed wire cages
in another part of the camp
where no one found them
and no one bothered to care.

"Hey Andrews. Want to go with us down
to Tudo tonight, grab some lobster,
smoke some dope, eat a little pussy?"

I have to go to bed early tonight.
I'm too tired to party,
too tired to read.
I hope the B-52s
don't keep me awake.

No more news tonight.
There is a tiger in my dreams.

UGLY PUSSY

This mama-san's ugly.
She's so ugly
that even the lifers
don't bother her.
She's got eyes like Uranus
and feet of grace.

As I try to sleep
after being on the perimeter all night,
she sweeps my area
and tells me about her family,
her brothers that have died,
her sisters that are whores in Saigon,
her mother that cries all day,
every day.

She tells me,
in broken English,
between broken teeth,
of the village she grew up in
that is now a napalmed, black grass plain.
She begins to shake as she talks,
like she's very, very cold.
I ask her into my cot,
under the blanket marked "U.S."
and hold her in my arms
until she stops shaking
and her breathing gets long
and warm, like a stream
flowing against my neck.

When I enter her
hours later
I don't think, even once,
about ugly or pretty,
I just feel lucky
to be real
if even for a short moment
between truth and hell,
and enjoy the
wet, warm of being.

MICHAEL ANDREWS

BODY COUNTS

They find them in the streets, drop them down wells
throw in a frag, and count the parts.

Lots and lots.

So many fingers and noses and elbows—
it's thirsty work winning hearts and minds,
counting all those thieves and lepers
and anything else that turns up dead
and now and then a real live dead Viet Cong
and any body with a hole in it.

Holes count.

Bullets make them, and grenades
and bayonets, claymores, bombs and bamboo;
knives poke them, axes hack them,
napalm burns them, worms eat them.
It all comes out the same:
put a hole in something and it leaks.

Put a hole in a body and it leaks.

If it leaks enough, it dies. Then you count it.
Simple, really.
Then you turn it into a lot of little pieces
and then you count the pieces and add.
Then you multiply by two.
Write down the answer to the nearest whole number
then you go away and you come back later
and you say, "My, my—It's Victor Charles"
and you count them up again.
Then it's just a matter of the proper channels.
The count goes to a lieutenant
who doubles it and gives it to a major
who doubles it and sends it on to Corps
who doubles it and adds it to a bigger list
and sends it on to MACV
where another Victor Charlie girl
doubles it and punches up the numbers on IBM cards
with a lot of little holes.

It's neat.
You can see how elegant the system is—
ashes to ashes, dust to dust, and holes to holes.

MICHAEL ANDREWS

The bodies turn into numbers and numbers are so tidy
something you can really get a handle on.
Then I create a system in the IBM
and it makes neat little reports.
The reports all report that we are winning the war
hands down.

I carry the reports over to Ambassador Bunker.
Listen, I say, we can win this war much faster
if we can just make the gooks smaller.
They're already tiny guys, but once we get them down
say, to the size of a hash mark
we can just paste the little buggers to the reports
like flies on paper, and save time and pencils
and especially Computer Time and you know
what Computer Time is costing, and the reports—
Cripes, I say, you can get the whole damn NVA
right there on your desk and spray
the little yellow pinkos with Raid.

Bunker says, Good thinking, but I have a better idea.
Why fuck with the little yellow bastards at all.
We just use numbers, see. We use Logic.
Let's say this number is a gook,
then we punch a hole in the number and count it up.
We can win this whole damn war right here in the Computer
then take the Computer someplace fun
like Pittsburgh.

That's what it takes to be an ambassador,
those kind of brains.

It makes everything so neat, so symbolic—
just like the Maoris in New Zealand;
when they want to have a war
they just meet between the two villages and slug it out
but if even one guy gets killed they stop the war.
Dying is against the rules.

The Aztecs had nothing against dying at all.
Some of the gods got indigestion eating the hearts
of common folk: virgins and children and such trash.
Since unhappy gods can make life a living hell
they needed to send up a few quality hearts from real
stand-up, square-shooting, straight-talking heroes.
So they had a limited war, and being cultured,
sensitive men, they called it the War of Flowers.

MICHAEL ANDREWS

You see, the concept of a limited war is nothing new.

A bunch of heroes got together and agreed to send
a bunch of other heroes out to punch holes in
a bunch of other heroes from the other side.
The heroes who leaked got to give their hearts to god.

This was a very great honor.

They threw the dying hero on a stone altar,
spread eagle, with a very pious priest at his head and
one on each arm and leg while the most pious priest of all
slashed his rib cage open in one, clean, swift cut
and tore his heart beating from his body
and threw it on the god's barbecue.

Imagine the happiness of such a hero.

It was very civilized in a very modern sort of way
because the whole population didn't have to go to war,
just the heroes.
If you didn't want to be a hero then
they just killed you with as much pain as they could
and you went to hell.

So when Ahuitzotl wanted to dedicate a temple to Tlaloc
he sent out his heroes on a two year campaign
and they collected 20,000 hearts to give to god.
They had not thought of both hearts and minds yet,
they were primitives, after all,
but they did collect ears.

Just imagine, 500 years later American heroes
played the same exact game, collecting and trading ears.

Tradition.

Imagine the piety of a man who would go
to all that trouble just to make god happy.

What's good for god is good for you.

It took them three days and three nights to punch
all the holes necessary to get those 20,000 hearts.
They had to work in shifts just like operators
in the modern computer facility

because their arms got tired tearing out the hearts.

And that's the beauty of the modern computer
it can punch all those holes in a matter of seconds.
And the wonderful thing about numbers and statistics
is that it makes everything so clear, so simple, so elegant.

It's so easy to see who is winning and who is losing.

Still, the Aztecs were very good indeed.
It took us an entire year to count 20,000 gook
hearts and minds in the Phoenix program.
The Aztecs got them all in three days.

By the way, we know that the Aztecs punched 20,000 holes
because some guy took the time

to count them.

DAVID WIDUP

THE FISH AND I

The fish in the shallow tidal pools
    of the South China Sea near Phan Rang
    swim slowly, the warm water almost
    the temperature of our own blood.

Standing waist deep, the dark blue and black
    fish swim between my legs, tails moving
    as if in slow motion, they seem to neither
    know or care what their next move will be.

Out to sea, the horizon falls off in a
    gentle curve in every direction.
    Blue sky meets dark blue ocean at a place
    these fish and I know we will never see.

They dive and scurry like wild electricity as
    the first bullets hit the water like the slap
    of Mother's hand hard against my face
    and I'm not sure whose blood turns the water red.

DEAR JOHN

I was lucky.
I didn't have a girlfriend when I went to Vietnam,
so I didn't get a Dear John letter.
But most of the guys did.

They started just weeks after we got there.
The "Johns" never came right out and said
"I've just been dumped by my old lady",
instead they'd drink all night
and take mescaline and speed and acid
all at once,
come back to the hutches
and throw their locker against the wall,
they'd shoot off clip after clip
of their M-16 at the black sky.
Bruce slammed his fist into the engine cover
of a deuce and a half
and shattered his hand.
It hung from his wrist like a wet towel.
Morton threw his reel to reel
against the wall until there was nothing left
except small pieces.
He put the pieces into his pillow case
and banged it against the wall
over and over and over again.

Most everybody got a letter.
Husbands, boyfriends, friends, sons.
Mothers left,
wives first fucked around - then left,
girlfriends left - then fucked around,
friends didn't write at all, or worse,
wrote to say how they hated us
for what we were doing.
Moms and Dads saw atrocities on TV
and wrote to say that they knew
we weren't doing the things they saw,
even though we did much worse
and dreamed of even more violent acts.

Schmidty, who taught me how to win at Hearts
gloated for most of ten months
about how he was going to come out of this,

his third year in hell over the last ten,
with wife and family intact.
He got his letter in August,
just six weeks before going home.
She ran away with his brother
whose wife left him
when he was in Nam
two years earlier.

He quit eating and sleeping.
A week later, I go with him
to Tuy Hoa to repair the hole
Charlie put in the perimeter fence,
the third time in my eleven months.
Schmidty heads up the construction,
me the security.
Two weeks into the job
and Schmidty is walking in the minefield every night.
I lose two ARVN guards trying to rescue him.
He walks out there with no clothes,
walking in a fucking minefield
and doesn't get shot
and doesn't blow up.
We med evac him out later on,
he's down to 135 pounds
and has circles under his eyes
you could mount on a jeep as tires.

SHORT TIMERS

SHORT TIMER   DAVID WIDUP

My squadron was unusual - we went over together and were all short together - so short we needed a ladder to climb up onto a dime, so short we had to look up to look down, so short we couldn't start anything for fear of not being able to finish it. Need to take a crap, but don't want to miss my plane. Want to smoke a cigarette, but don't want to waste half of it. Like to get laid, but don't want to pay for nothing.

Short was less than 100 days left in country. Short meant FIGMO (Fuck it, got my orders.) Short timers had their own culture, their own set of rules. Some slept in bunkers for the last 99 nights, afraid the first rocket in would catch them sleeping. Many stopped alcohol and drugs to keep sharp. Those that had started out fucking everything they could, ended worrying about the clap and VD. Almost everyone who was going to take R&R - that one week of respite out of the country in Hong Kong, Australia, Thailand, Hawaii - had already taken it. There was nothing else to look forward to but getting home.

I was crazy for 100 days. I was sure I was going to die. In my last 100 days, I was stoned most of the time, flew an airplane for kicks, went up in a Huey gunship in the middle of a rocket attack and flew to almost every RED HORSE location in Nam. I was sure I was going to die. I thought about extending for another seven months, but didn't. I quit writing home. As a short timer, I mostly hurt from head to toe - afraid to stay and afraid to go.

STARS & STRIPES
in war the first casualty is the truth — **Aeschylus**

In the Pacific *Stars & Stripes*
Lt. Calley was just doing his job,
there is a chicken in the pot of every
free market, democracy loving citizen
of South Vietnam, there is only goodness in our hearts
and that someone named Nixon
gets to speak in my name.

It is also the final toilet
for the world's worst poetry.
The truly bad poetry is okay
with me, even the rhymers
and the bad greeting card verse
riddled with cliches and wrong words.

At least it isn't as infantile as the Rod
McKuen poem I keep above my desk to
remind me that things can always get worse.

No sense reading the Stripes for news.
That comes straighter from *Newsweek*
or *Ramparts* and down the rumor trail.
It does tell me when *Mission Impossible*
is on American Forces TV in Pleiku.
It is often sandwiched between *Star Trek*
and *The Monkees* and is often printed
just below the weekly bikini girl
wearing the Jacki Kennedy hairdo
and a smile only the suicidal would
slip his dick into.

Mostly the Stripes is used to wrap bread and fish
by the local free market entrepreneurs.
And when I am under siege by dysentery
or the PX is out of reliable toilet paper
it is better than tin foil and wax paper.
Always remember to crumple it well.
It's softer that way and wipes away
more of what it is designed to spread.
Try to use older, outdated copies
otherwise the inky fabrications
may still be too wet, and there you are
walking around all day with the major
lies of our times printed on your ass.

LAOS

The *Stars and Stripes* says
"Nixon promises no war in Laos!"

I stand in the Aerial Port,
on my way to Nah Trang,
and there's a line of grunts
a mile long,
a snake full of killing evil,
waiting in line.

I've never seen a line like this,
in eleven months,
and ask a friendly looking,
blond grunt,
"What's happening?"
He says,
"Laos"
and spits at my feet,
looks the other way
so I know he's had enough
of talking about the War.

They all died.
Every one of them died,
before anyone knew they were there.

JERRY TABASKI LEAVES TOWN

Tabaski had seen it all through his fat lenses.
Tabaski was one of the decent guys
and he'd been in country for two years too long
and when he'd seen the students arrested,
the whores stealing,
the whores beaten,
the cripples from Con Son,
the White Mice's petty graft,
the big time graft of President Thieu,
the beggars that cheat,
the beggars that die,
the incompetence of the military,
U.S. and otherwise,
the fundamental lies
spitting from the computer,
the dead and the wounded
and the traumatic amputees
at Third Field Hospital,
the greed, venality and stupidity
of his fellow expatriots,
the rape and theft and murder
and he's made enough of a little nest egg
Tabaski decides it is time to leave town.

But Tabaski just isn't going to fly
back to Small Town US of A
with its greasy bacon and eggs
and the hearty yahoos
of its brain dead jingoists.
He has plans to take a ship
right out of the Saigon harbor
and sail through island paradises,
Bali, Indonesia, Java — who knows
where a guy might find a taste of sanity
and a mirror to practice forgiveness in.

He says good-bye to all of us
dumb enough to stay behind,
ships out his possessions
and pack his suitcase for good times.
He gets up at 5 AM, coffees up
and starts walking from his apartment
to the Saigon River where he gets
the small boat to the freighter
that is taking him as away as away can get.

MICHAEL ANDREWS

He's wrestling his big suitcase
in one hand and his small one in the other
down Tudo Street toward freedom
when some desperado, a Saigon cowboy
points a serious looking .45
at Tabaski, "I take watch, all money.
Now," the cowboy shouts
in the dead empty dusk of another day
of pillage, burn, torture and rape.

Tabaski blinks through his thick glasses.
It takes a moment to realize that this
is Vietnam's last little joke
and he bursts out laughing,
head back, shoulders shaking
belly laughing right in the guy's face
and he just brushes the gun aside
and walks on down Tudo,
laughing all the way to the Saigon River.

Some months later, Tabaski sends us
a postcard from one paradise or another
and tells us the story of his happy escape.

It does not mention the mirror,
or even peace of mind.

I never heard from Tabaski again.

READING THE LAMPOON

The Majors all hate me more than anyone
else they hate and more than anyone else hates me
because I have long hair, an attitude and I outrank them
and Ambassador Bunker hates me because
I won't prove they are winning the war on green bar
computer paper with neat perforations along the side
and the bosses hate me because I am the best
programmer that ever darkened their door
but I'm more or less out of control
and the CIA guys from Phoenix hate me
because I have Chairman Mao books on my desk
and a poster that says I'd rather be red than dead
and the grunts in green hate me because
I make good money, wear civies
and have a woman with round eyes
and I don't take shit from Majors
and the old men expatriots hate me because
I'm young and I have a woman with round eyes
and the Vietnamese hate me because
I'm an American imperialist with too much money
and the whores hate me because
I have a woman with round eyes
and I am saving too much money
and the French expatriots hate me because
I can't speak French and they hate everyone in general
and the brain-dead flag wavers
who love war hate me because I don't
and because I say so and because I think it's silly
but I do have a few friends.

Also, I'm not entirely sane anymore.
I've most definitely been in country too long
and some gear has slipped between my ears
and I say unkind things about President Nixon
and the idea of Vietnamization
and I have a satirical attitude toward uniforms
and a cynical one about anybody's authority
and everyone who hates me and everyone that doesn't
knows I can't last much longer.

In the PX I get the November 1970 National Lampoon
because it is saner than anything we make the computer
spit up and because it has a 1896 Sears Roebuck Sex Catalog
and because I need a laugh and because it pisses off
the grunt who sells it to me and who hates me

MICHAEL ANDREWS

because I can read without moving my lips.

When I get it back to the office I start reading
a farce on macho men's magazines and war horseshit
called "The Dink Patrol and the Love Slaves of Xuyen Tan Phu."
In two paragraphs I'm out of control, running
between the desks full of drunk or dozing programmers
up to the front where I find Flo and Linda
actually trying to earn their salaries
and where all the Majors hang around
like hall monitors hoping someone will drop
a combat medal or a fifth of vodka
and I scream, "Listen to this,"
choking on my words because I can't stop
the insane guffawing and belly laughing
and I stomp up and down the office reading out loud
about the slaughter of every man, woman and child
in an unarmed village because they were dink terrorist
and about raping the women because they really wanted it
and then killing them because they were spies
and how hard it is to target a toddler
and how dangerous frail old men armed with false teeth are
and how disgusting cowards are groveling in the dirt
begging for their lives and how the hero
has to protect himself from the little kid
begging for chocolate by firing a warning shot
right between his eyes
and how the mothers used their own infants
as human shields but the hero sees through
that old trick and shoots them both anyway
and how the Cong use tiny soldiers
just because they make bad targets
and how the hero has to chase the Geneva Convention Observer
through the jungle and kill him in brutal hand to hand combat
and just to make sure he cuts off his head
and when he gets back to the demolished village
the medic asks, "Are you okay, chaplain?"
and this is where I lay down on the floor
and laugh until I choke green and blue
and the programmers go back to dozing
and Flo and Linda conspire how to save me
from myself and the majors start plotting
on how to get my name on a Phoenix hit list.

All afternoon I chuckle about that dumb Lampoon article
and wait for the clock to turn me loose.
The fact is I'm insane.

I know why nobody loves me.
I really don't hate anybody at all.
How dumb can you get.

MICHAEL ANDREWS

BUYING BALLOONS
NOV 27, 1970

It's Flo's birthday and the afternoon monsoon
has blown past. It leaves a bit of cool
and treacherous mud puddles on Hoang Dieu.
I am walking to Hasty Tasty,
across Cach Mang to get us dinner,
the best elephant hamburgers made
in this dandy little war.
I round the corner by the Saigon Milk Bar
where the whores are singing
along with 'Hey Jude'
and a half block from #14, our villa,
a brother-sister team are walking away
from the sunset, hustling balloons
tied up on a five foot stick
like two trolls going to repair a rainbow.
The balloons have tails tied
out of top secret printouts,
hot off the printers at MAVC
with secrets that were printed in Newsweek
two editions ago and the whole
balloon tree is only fifty cents MPC.
I take their picture walking in the mud
with the fading day at their backs
and the rainbow on their shoulders.

It's Flo's birthday so I buy the whole bunch.
Fifty cents—they screwed me and they knew it.
They screwed me and I didn't care.
After all, I got the picture.
I bring them home to Flo and I get Flo's smile.
I take another picture of Flo in the back
yard, under the banana tree and the cistern,
making the peace sign with a rainbow on her shoulder.

Not a bad night in hell—
the kids made their fortune,
Flo is all smiles and balloons,
I'll get lucky in bed—

rainbows out of mud.

XMAS GOES TO WAR

Lights on the tree, flares in the night,
I am sweating in the bed
while the windows buzz from the bombs.

"Merry Xmas Laos," I say
and listen to the whine of the mosquitoes.

Santa Claus is coming to town
in a two-stroke cyclo
crazy as a mama-san
cheated for an all-night girl.
Green uniforms and red uniforms,
they all look like generals to me.
I send the maid out for a tree.
The locals are obliged to cheat a round-eye.
We fill it up with lights and bulbs
that we buy in the central market,
and tinsel that Pop sends us from the world.

We are trying to stay sane.

We strip down to underwear
and sweat out the night.
We pile up the gifts from home
and from Hong Kong
and from each other.

Flo never wants to make love
and I never want anything else.
The fortunes of war.
We are at war too.
And in love and in pain
and fear drips icicles at 95 degrees.

The body boxes are stacked and waiting
at the Ton Son Nhut morgue,
waiting for that last sleigh ride home.

"Merry Xmas World," I say.

"Fuck it," I say, and drive on
downtown, dodging whores and deuce-and-a-halfs,
change money with mama-san in the tea-bar,
give my liquor ration to a friendly wino.
I am waiting for the knife, the bomb,

MICHAEL ANDREWS

the blind, random shot.

"Like a bridge over troubled waters"
wails from a tea-bar.
I bring candles home to Flo.

We light them up and open gifts.
We lay in bed sweating
too hot to touch,
holding hands.
It is good enough
to be alive.

THE MISSING GUNS

Inspection.
Armory inventory.
JAG Investigation.
I've got the right number of guns,
400 M-16s,
45 M-60s,
30 M-79 Grenade launchers,
36 .38s,
8 .45s.
But four of the M-16s have the wrong serial numbers.
I can't go home until I get the right ones back.
Three months left.

I know where they're at,
Cam Rahn Bay
or Phan Rang
or Tuy Hoa
or Da Nang
or any one of thirty little,
chickenshit, Army LZs
we built towers or pads on.

I fly on C-123s
from Bien Hoa
to Pleiku to Phan Rang.
The guns aren't in the Armory.
Jonesy thinks there at Can Rahn.
We drink beer and smoke a joint.
When he came over,
he wanted to be a cop
when he got back to the world.
Now he wants to sell drugs.

The next morning,
I fly on another C-123 to Cam Rahn Bay.
The plane is filled with Vietnamese,
they're scared,
some puke on the 25 minute flight,
others huddle in groups of three and four,
arms around each other.
I can't stand it,
go up front with the pilot,
he talks me through the final approach,
smoking a joint and laughing.
At the last minute he takes over.

He had me landing the wrong way.
He's still laughing.
I'm shaking,
89 days left
and I'm landing airplanes.

Walking from the Aerial Port at Cam Rahn
to our compound,
I'm stopped by a AP,
he's wearing stateside fatigues,
they're starched.
I wonder what happened to the war.
He pulls out his .38
and tells me to spread eagle on the road.
I tell him to fuck himself
and walk away.
He runs after me screaming,
seems they don't allow guns
on the Air Base.
I wonder what happened to the war.

Three of the missing M-16s are here,
in the Cam Rahn Red Horse Armory.
I tell them to ship them to Bien Hoa,
leave my guns in the Armory
and ask directions to hospital.
It's a long walk,
I'm tired and hot when I finally get there.
It takes over an hour to find
Hindermann and Ugly,
my buddies from stateside
I'd been with Ugly since Basic.

They work nights,
I had to wake them up,
in their air conditioned huts,
I wonder what happened to the war.
We smoke dope and I sleep hard,
wake up after dark,
don't know where I'm at.
I get some water and look around Hindy's area.
He's a Medic,
hospital shit all over the place,
scalpels, surgical gloves, whites.
I play his guitar
before finding the note.
"Grab some food at the Mess Hall,

meet me in Post-Op #5."
No directions.
I find the Mess Hall,
Ugly cooks me some eggs.
He tells me not to go to Post-Op,
says Hindy's kind of flipped out,
has gotten obsessive about blood and guts.
I get directions to Post-Op #5 anyway.

It's a long hut
a corrugated metal half circle
with wood floors.
There are ten or fifteen of them,
connected by a covered walkway.
It's raining now.
They say it rains in Cam Rahn every night
during monsoon season.
It's dark inside,
I have to squint to see.
Hindy shows me the patients.
Some are American,
some ARVN,
some North Vietnamese.
They're all in pieces,
missing arms, legs, chests, faces.
I can't believe they are alive.
I notice the smell,
ask Hindy what it is,
he smiles, says "burnt flesh."
He wants to show me all these people,
pull back sheets,
remove gauze
and explain their wounds.
One guy gets serious,
flopping around, groaning.
the Medics all run that way,
I leave quietly,
walk to the Aerial Port.

I'm shaking as I get on the plane
back to Bien Hoa
the next morning.
I vomit on the flight.
I lie and tell Sgt. Bigelow
I found all four guns
in the Cam Rahn Armory.
He tells me they found one

while I was gone.
The exposed lie means nothing to me.
I just look at him and shrug.
"Don't mean nothin."
he says and walks away.

WILLY PETER

"It fuckin' goes right through ya,"
Vinny shrieks at Peacenik
while his hands shake and fumble
at the compress wrapper
and Dinky watches a cloud
sail past the green, leafy canopy
his eyes have just faded away
the picture of the star burst
the white phosphorous blooming
like a time lapsed movie
of a fireworks flower
unfolding to the sun.

A case a friendly fire
his mind rolls around slowly.
The air strike was too close,
but then so was Charley
and he can hear Vinny screaming
about it goes right through ya
and he guesses that it has
something to do with him
but the cloud is somehow
the most profound thing that
he has ever seen, way beyond
the merely beautiful,
the way it drifts,
a galleon charting the seas
of heaven and he can feel
Vinny pushing on his chest
and the sucking way he breathes
but in the end
the cloud just
takes him
away.

MICHAEL ANDREWS

THE ROOT CANAL

The lower right molar explodes like
a slow motion fragmentation grenade
and when it hurts so bad I can't sleep all night
I try to get a dentist at Third Field Hospital
but they won't touch an American civilian,
just corrupt Vietnamese officials
so I have to get drilled on the economy.
I find a lady Vietnamese dentist
in Cholon who says she got her degree at USC
and she talks better English than
the best of the tea bar girls,
but then degrees are only as far
as the nearest print shop.

She is only a 70 pound Vietnamese woman,
soaking wet with a drill in each hand.
How could she be a threat to a 180 pounds
of supremely conditioned American male?
She says the tooth has to have a root canal
and a crown and that she can do that
and that's the good news.

"Okay," I groan, taking many oaths
about never taking another drink of Coca-Cola,
"what's the bad news?"

"There is no novacaine in Vietnam right now."

Now I know there is a god.
She is a salacious idiot,
a malicious troglodyte.
She is not an American
and she wakes up every morning
and wonders, "Just what can I do
today to fuck up this guy Andrews."

I sink back into the antique dentist rack,
resigned to my shit-soaked karma.
"Okay," I whisper, "do it."
The drills are old and clatter like jack hammers
and she grinds down into the impacted tooth
like a Texan capitalist sniffing for oil.
The sweat pops out of my forehead,
so many beads on a waxed bathtub
and I go red all over trying not to scream

MICHAEL ANDREWS

and my fingers begin to have serious intentions
about crushing the steel arm rest
and then she stops, packs the cavern
with wads of cotton and says,
"Three days you come back,
less pain and nerve more dead.
You drink whiskey maybe, easier for you."

"Thanks," I mutter, prying
each finger lose one at a time,
"I don't drink," and I crawl outside
to the Honda car and pay off the kid
who acts as my hired gun, guaranteeing
not to steal the car while
I listen to the whir of drill
and pray for an easy death.

Three days later the throbbing air-strike
in my skull is less than megatonnage
and she pulls the cotton and says,
"This will hurt, just very short time,"
and my fingers find their prints
on the steel arm rest and grip.
She has a very tiny wood awl,
just like the one I use for boring holes
in a door for a knob, only
it's just bigger than a toothpick
and she plunges it down into the tooth
already detonated with cold water,
finds the meat of the nerve
and screws it in while my vision
goes to black with stars, twists and yanks
and I am just rounding Pluto on the way
for a little chat with god
when she jerks out a little piece of pink meat
that only moments ago was my nerve
and is probably even now screaming
it's own message to a brain
that is no longer taking calls
and just when I know that life has
moments of nearly terminal pain
it stops and I sag back into the chair
whimpering slightly, "shoot me,
don't send me home like this."

She packs the tooth again and tells me
with great compassion, "Next time easier for you,"

and right then I know she is telling
me the good lie, and that she is VC.
She is making a few bucks and saving novacaine
to send out to the tunnels in Cu Chi
for some guy who has to get his leg
sawed off with just a hit of rice wine
and maybe a bit of local anesthesia.

I mop off the sweat, stagger out
to the VC kid waiting for his cut
and three days later I'm back
because life is simply filled
to the brim with those tiny mirages of choice
that are never really there
and we do it all over again
only this time deeper, going for
the root of that nerve that never
hurt another living thing
and she most certainly lied
because this time the pain
achieves a kaleidoscope of bursting
colors right behind my eyeballs
and she whispers the way a lover
does after a bad night, "Next time
last time, not so much pain,"
and I love her for the lie
and pay off the kid whose smile
is free of dental worry
and whose belly could eat the world.

But this time she told me true
and after some average pain
of super human intensity
she makes the mold and one week later
I am in the chair with my fingers
pressed into their individual dents
and the only pain is the dry, cold
air blowing out the canyon
that used to be my tooth
and the beautiful gold crown
gets hammered in place.
She steps back from the strapado,
smiles at her work and me and says, "Fini.
You brave man Mr. Michael,"
and for that moment we know we are
bonded forever, like lovers,
in the web of pain that sews us all

into the same quilt
and I pry up my fingers
and I smile back as I pay her in green dollars.
It's the least I can do for that guy in the tunnels.
I give up Coca-Cola for iced tea
and the kid takes home his final payment.

ROCK 'N ROLL WAR

Someone on the line yells Rock 'N Roll
and every motherfucker not stoned blind
slips his weapon to full auto and lets
it fly, no one aims except away,
except at the jungle green fear,
across interlocking fields of fire
they scream and spray the tracers
and the ones no can see but anyone
can hear except for the guy
who inherits his karma
and they squeeze that trigger tight
until the chambers spit up empty
and the belts drop limp into the mud
and the last chamber coughs up dry
and no one can focus on much of anything
because their eyes are crazy
and fuzzy with the fear and anxious
to see that nothing very bad is going to happen
and when it doesn't, they stand down,
lapse into the dull torpor, brains
as vacant as an empty casing
and they switch on the tape player
and the Stones leap out to fill
up the air, because if there is music,
if there is simply noise
if there is anything but silence
then we must all be alive.

And the music is everywhere.
It is how we know that we are not officers.
It is how we know that we have homes to go to.

I find Joni Mitchel in the PX
and I like her picture on the cover
and a song with the title "Michael From Mountains,"
and I take it home to Flo
and we sing it all night long
while the geckos dance on the wall
and the mosquitoes cruise for a snack
and the roaches and the ants
assault the cupboards.

I got Dylan and the Beatles
and Vivaldi and Simon & Garfunkle
and it floats out of the tea bars

off scratchy LPs and from the wild
time night clubs, from the Filipino Bands
wailing "Hey Jude" and the pelvis grinding
singers raise every pecker in the room
and the sweet, tight miniskirts
reveal a bit of panties,
the sweet fold of an ass
and just a flash of pussy
while she fucks a microphone and mimics
"Mother Mary Comes To Me."

Without the music we'd all be lifers
as dead from scrotum to skull
as a burnt out lump of charcoal.

And sometimes when the night is long
and there is no one around
and I am sure the doors and windows are secure
I put on Simon & Garfunkle and they
chant "a time of innocence,"
and without an ounce of fucking shame

I let the tears drool down my empty face.

DAVID WIDUP

THE BUNKERS

At the end of our tour of duty,
we lay on top of the sand filled bunkers
rotting from the inside out
(like everything else in this godforsaken country)
to get a tan.

We feel the need to go home looking
like we've been in a tropical paradise,
even though all we have done
for the past year is sleep in the day
and wander around in the jungle at night.
Or, some have wandered around the jungle in the day,
but not in a way that gets us very tan,
so now that we are short timers
(so short we need a ladder to climb up on a dime),
we lay on top of these bunkers
and ask the sun to make us look
like our lives have been different this past year.

The radio blares "Chrystal Blue Persuasion"
and "Lay Lady, Lay" and other oddments of reason
from a time turned upside down
while we lay on these bunkers
thinking a lot about what's at home,
will the girls still be there and
will they want to be with us and
will the car run and
what will it be like to be safe again and
how many times will it take before I wake up without a hard on and
will I ever get enough real food back in this stomach and
how about my friend Joe who said he'd never speak to me again
if I went to Vietnam even though we spent years in school together,
doubledated at the Junior Prom with the Hasburt twins
and I was the pulling guard on the football team
for him for two years and saved his ass
from getting knocked silly by dumb jocks
looking to be a hero by taking Joe's head off
and stealing the football.
I wonder if Joe will speak to me.

It's hot on top of these bunkers
looking for a tan to go home with and
hoping it will be worthwhile.

TIES

It's 99% humidity
and 99% pacified
and 99 degrees in the shade
and it's raining
and it's raining bullets
and it's raining sweat
and it's raining tears
and the Generals
who are losing the war
want our bosses
who have lost their minds
to tell us
who have lost our souls
to wear ties to work
where no one can see us
in the cold fog
of the air conditioned
cigarette smoke
and the green meat
of the fluorescent lights.

Now we know we have lost the war.
They have built white picket fences
and they want spit-shined civilians
and they want ties.

They tell us that we are
capital P Professionals.
When professionals lose
they lose with decorum.

Most guys fall into their ties
like a pig in shit
and they don't care as long as
the pussy doesn't dry up
and the pay checks roll in.

But Mike Brown can't stand it
any more than I can
and he finds the world's ugliest tie,
green, red and puce
and he dips it in mustard and catsup
for politically correct stains
and crusts it up with
beany weanies and when he

picks his nose
he wipes the buggers
where a tie pin ought to be.

I can't beat that
so when the memo comes my way that says
that I have been naughty
about wearing a proper uniform and a tie
and that they are serious about this
I find a piece of acetate and cut
out an invisible tie
and put it around a blue chambray
work shirt with a collar
with a ring inside the neck
and strangle myself with a rubber band.
I take a red grease pencil and
down the front of the tie
I write in big block letters
   T
   I
   E
so it has an appropriate design
and so the generals will know whose side I'm on
and the bosses
will have their asses covered
and their necks in a noose.

It just won't cut it
and Control Data Corporation
writes me an official memo
that defines the concept of tie
as excluding acetate and
grease pencils of any color
and in the end I have to send
away to the Sears and Roebuck catalog
for a huge bow tie
with bright, hallucinogenic colors
and just a proper dose of fuck you.

Old Benjamin almost got it right—
in the end it's death and it's taxes
and it's tow the line.
So never spit into the wind.
Don't rock the boat.
Be a team player
and never let your tie
clash with the tie

of the guy that
tap dances on your face.

Today's forecast is—
14 KIA,
38 wounded,
4,237 neutralized enemies
and 1 AWOL somewhere
between the ears.

OATMEAL COOKIES

They were in the Central Highlands around 67,
Green Berets, living native with the Montagnards.
In one village, if you didn't sleep with the chief's
daughter they boiled you up for lunch.
In another village, five miles down the river
if you even looked at the chief's daughter
they turned you into salted pork.

There was always someone trying to turn them
into mulch at the bottom of a compost heap.
If the dysentery and malaria didn't kill you
then bad food, bullets or a snake did.
If you lived through that you might get R&R
in Bangkok, and an incurable dose of the clap.

They hadn't seen their girls for two years
and so the pay didn't matter,
but the little things counted:
staying alive until sunset, letters from home,
a can of fruit cocktail and dry socks.

They had a pet honey bear named Pepper.
She was more than just something to do.
She lived in a tree at the edge of camp
and she came down for oatmeal cookies
and those fruit cakes that came by the ton
every time Christmas rolled through the jungle.
But most of all, Pepper loved to wrestle
and box and hug and scratch.
She'd stand up on her hind legs
and hang her stomach way out
hoping that someone would come along
and take a couple of punches at it
so they could box and wrestle
and eat more oatmeal cookies.

Pepper loved those oatmeal cookies.
She was the only thing in the jungle
that did not belong to the enemy.
And Pepper did not belong to the army.
Pepper belonged to the grunts
and she was the only living thing in the jungle
that wasn't trying to kill them.
Pepper was someone a grunt could trust
and when she begged to have her fur scratched

she stood between the grunts and
the black edge of madness.

No one could deny that Sergeant Adams was a prick.
He wanted spit-shined jungle boots and clean latrines.
He liked to send the greenest men into
the most dangerous places. He liked to piss
in the Montagnards rice cache.
What he liked best was to see how many grunts
he could piss off in a day.
He was not a happy man as sergeants go
and one day he got as drunk as bees on fermented honey
and he shot Pepper full of M-16 holes.

That day he pissed everyone off.

Nobody said a word, they just went off
and cleaned their weapons.
Someone buried Pepper so
the Montagnards wouldn't eat her.

Four days later a patrol found Sergeant Adams
swinging in a tree, as dead as a clean latrine
with an oatmeal cookie stuffed in his mouth.

Although Mrs. Adams had had a different husband
every week since she forgot about the Sergeant
the Army shipped her the remains

plus regrets.

MICHAEL ANDREWS

THE FIRE ANT OFFENSIVE
GIA DINH, SAIGON, 1969

The Fire ants have infiltrated our bathroom;
Red Hordes marching in long columns
along Ho Chi Minh trails in the plumbing
and through breaches in the wall.
Their first assault comes after the monsoons,
a traditional time for offensive action.
I turn off the shower and towel down
and suddenly I am on fire from head to crotch.
There is nothing like a fire ant bite.
They burn and sting and itch all at the same time.
They don't go away for days and days.
I jump back under the shower, rinse away
the fire and watch them swirl down the drain.
The fire ants set up ambushes in towels
waiting for a moron to take a shower.
When they bite me below the belt I declare war.
The next day I am back with 105mm Raid cans,
but they are insidious, and persistent.

Only an idiot forgets to shake out his towel.

I see now that their real objective
is to destroy the economy of the food cabinet.
Taking full advantage of the natural cover
small units hit the sugar bowl and vanish
before effective countermeasures can be mounted.
I find hundreds of the little red bastards
drowned and fermenting in the honey bowl.
I could tolerate the beans, rice, bread and fruit
but an attack on my honey is an attack against
the very heart of my freedom and sovereignty.
I set the legs of the cabinet in coffee cans
and then I fill the cans with water.
It is both a moat and a defensive perimeter.
Although I cannot seek out and destroy the enemy
in the jungles of the bathroom and the weeds of the yard,
I will control the countryside by defending
the central areas of commerce and resources.
At times I sprinkle a little sugar on the floor,
just enough to tease them into action,
then I sit on the cool tile and squash them,
one at a time, chuckle and total up the score.
I will win because all the honey is mine by right

and because I have superior technology and fire power.

By Tet, the reds have learned how to build
pontoon bridges with burnt out match sticks.

I am in the shower with my towel shaken out,
my Raid cans, the fly swatter and jungle boots.
Flo is in the kitchen, in command of KP duty.
I am daydreaming about a world free of ants
and safe for honey, rice and bananas.
Suddenly Flo screams "Omygod, they're in the rice.
We have to go out for dinner."
I rinse the last Freddy Able down the drain.
Freddy Able is code talk for the FA.
FA is short for the dreaded Fire Ant hordes.
I stalk, cautiously, into the kitchen zone.
"Nonsense," I say. "If we let the kitchen fall
the living room might be next.
God knows, they may even take the bedroom."
I place the huge fan on the floor and turn it on.
The blades are beating the air, whap whap whap,
I am flushed with the excitement of going into battle.
I pour out the rice and ants in front of the fan.
The rice falls straight down but it blows
the ants across the room, where their little
red bodies smash into the wall.

"The specific gravity of rice, my dear,
is greater than that of the ants."

I sweep up the rice and while I wait for dinner
I mop up the operation and squash stragglers.

I love science.

I am not afraid of the night.

AERIAL PORT
OUTGOING
BIEN HOA

The fuckers delayed my flight two days,
nightmares of dying on day 366 or 367
consume me, black is everywhere.
I rebel and move into the Aerial Port on day 365.
Screw 'em,
I'm staying here until I get on a freedom bird.

It's not a building -
it's a concrete pad with a thin steel roof.
No walls, no rooms.
I'm parked with my duffel bag
against an I beam.

All the GIs here look like teenagers.
The sun pours in like orange juice.
I see pistols in the hands of all the gooks,
but they disappear when I look close.
It's cold in here today.
The air is heavy and wet.
It won't go into my lungs.

Spiders the size of footballs
wrap me in marijuana leaf.
It's smoking, my flesh is on fire.
I stare at the sofa my mother died on.
It's a green brocade with a small cigarette hole
in one of the arms.
The spiders cover my eyes with a fur coat.
It's not even warm enough.
My lungs fill with ice.
The spiders grow into soldiers with owl's heads.
They try to carry me away.

Jimmy Scarpati shakes me awake.
"Come on, man,
get back to the barracks."
I don't say a word,
just shake hard and light a cigarette.
Drumskin reverberates thinly.
It's dark outside.
I cannot see anything,
anything beyond the edge of the pad.

I hear the sirens bleat like a castrated pig,
but nobody is running for the bunkers.
I look at Jimmy, he's just smiling at me.
The sirens get louder,
only I can hear them.

In the bunker by myself,
I hang the duffel bag on a hook
and lay on the wet, rotting bench.
The sirens haven't stopped.
Pigs fill the bunker,
big fat ones with ugly snouts
the size of pie tins.
They smell like burnt flesh.
They come in a slow moving line,
one after the other.
They keep coming in even after it's full.
I think they must be hiding
in the sandbags.
Willows fill my brain,
I lose my virginity once again.
I am floating in the South China Sea
when the machine gun blasts into the water,
Condon gets hit, is bleeding Kool Aid,
but keeps swimming, smiling at the sun.

Jimmy shakes me hard.
I slip off the bench.
He's got the new CO with him,
.45 strapped around his waist.
"Your ass is in LBJ now, motherfucker.
Fuck with me, you won't ever
get back to the world."
I open my mouth to scream
and vomit until my stomach comes out.

Jimmy comes and finds me
an hour before our plane takes off.
He carries me and Joe drags my duffel bag with his.
On the plane, I pray for the first time in years,
pray to a God I don't love,
to please let me sleep, let this plane get off.

MICHAEL ANDREWS

BODY BAGS

    for the 5th Cavalry to the tune of *Camptown Ladies Sing This Song*

The 5th Cavalry had a hell of a good time
with the new guys who got shipped in by the planeload
walking on their own two boots, the green grunts,
the boys with the clear eyes, clear skin, clear consciencenesses.
They would have a barbecue, part of the on-the-job-training,
learning to laugh at death like real men;
six-by loads of PX beer and roasted hot-dogs
and they would all get drunk together
and they would laugh and chuckle and swig the suds,
and they would wear these silly cowboy hats
so they all looked just like Custer riding to his last stand,
and they would put their arms around one another
and they would sway back and forth, back and forth, singing
    you're going home in a body bag
    do-dah
    do-dah.

And they would.

They would chopper out to the boonies
and three weeks later they would come back,
and they would come back only two ways;
in a body bag
or out.

And the ones that were 'out' weren't green anymore,
and they didn't wear the silly cowboy hats, and they never laughed,
or they laughed too loud or at the wrong things,
and they never sang and they still drank the PX beer,
but their eyes looked to infinity or they jerked all over the place,
and their skins turned into roadmaps of hell,
all lines and roads and intersections and stop signs,

and their hair sometimes turned white,
and they got old, not wise,
and not real men,
just old.

And the ones that were 'in' the body bags were just dead.
They never even got old; just dead,
and they died in ones and twos

and by the baker's dozen, by the gross, and by the ton.
And they put them in the bags and rushed them to the freezers
before they turned black and rotten and the bags would fill up
with stinking gas like balloons that someone forgot to color.
And they didn't sing anymore,
and they didn't get the PX beer either,
but they got their wish

    you're going home in a body bag
    do-dah
    do-dah.

Every night I sweat in bed
whether or not Flo lets me have the air-conditioner on.
Flo hates the air-conditioner, but I sweat.
It's always hot and hotter and everything rots;
books and shoes and food and bodies, and the pillow that I sweat into.
Even when the air-conditioner is freezing I rot in my sleep
and Flo says that I grind my teeth so hard that the noise wakes her up
even above the conditioner and the B-52s and the bombs,
and I say, "It's the stink, the pillows are rotting."

So one day I got some body bags
and put them on the pillows to keep them dry.
Flo said, "Oh, where did you get the plastic bags."
I said, "They're body bags" and she tore it off
and said that she couldn't sleep on it.
"Jesus," I said, "they're just big goddamn plastic baggies."
But after a few nights the sweat would just lay in puddles,
and the bags made noise when the bombs would plow up the night,
and I tossed and turned, grinding my teeth,
and the body bags would crinkle and pop
like they were singing some song I've heard before.
But the worst part is that they would sigh, whooosh,
like gas leaking from a balloon,
like they were trying to breath for someone
who couldn't catch their breath
from too much laughing or too much singing.
And no one is singing anymore
because we are all in some kind of body bag.

And that's the difference I guess:
outside the bag you can still hear the bombs
and the crinkle and the breathing and the singing,

MICHAEL ANDREWS

and inside the bag
you never hear
a goddamn thing.

      do-dah
      do-dah.

IN THE WORLD

BACK IN THE WORLD — MICHAEL ANDREWS

By now I had amassed enough savings by not throwing it away on booze, whores, dope and parties to be able to afford the luxury of a righteous dose of indignation. When the bullshit outweighs the dollars it is time to go. Open rebellion ensues. Stupidity, graft, brutality, corruption, degeneracy, sadism, violence, murder, rape, greed, incompetence, imperialism, theft, fear and anger held no more lessons for me.

I could no longer keep my mouth shut and follow orders.

The World is what everyone in Vietnam except the Vietnamese called Hometown, US of A in particular, and everywhere else but the Nam in general. The World was a mythical place, a fantasy land of dreams come true, of life fulfilled, of easy Saturday mornings, camping trips, fast cars, loving women and real hamburgers. We lived for The World, for coming Home to peace and joy, love and understanding, to simple pleasures, the pursuit of harmless dreams and real Christmas trees. We knew The World waited for us to come home to a thing called sanity.

When I got fired and I also quit and we were on the way to The World, we first went to Hong Kong. One last shopping trip. Honk Kong had lost its charm. It had transformed from a loving and eager whore to a mendacious and venal pimp. The Green Machine was getting out of town and like any whipped bully, it was taking its marbles with it.

The Hong Kong economy and the local merchants had come to rely on a steady flow of green dollars via The Green Machine and courtesy of the American taxpayer. It was no longer friendly. It was no longer fun.

We were there for one last emergency shopping safari. Even the Star Ferry had lost its joy.

After leaving Vietnam, Flo and I traveled around the world looking for sanity and peace. It was my thinking that we could sit on the beach in Perth Australia and wash the war away. In twenty years of living in the world of facts, the Nam has never left me for a single day.

It is my feeling that humans are more related to one another than they are alien. We wandered around the world by bus and train and ship and plane and finally, by VW bus. Like Diogenes I was searching, not so much for the Good Man, but for a Good People, a Good Culture, and Good Geography. I was searching for a way to escape an America gone insane. I was, and still am convinced that every dollar earned, every dollar spent, and every dollar of tax paid is a form of rape. I wanted to find a quiet, sane place to become a self subsistent farmer. I also wanted to give Advaita Vedanta, monasticism and mysticism one last look in India. I wanted to see the world. It took a year. I found both human empathy and inhuman chauvinism—nothing new. And so, somewhat to my surprise, we ended up back in a place called The World or, sometimes, Home.

Somewhere going over the Khyber Pass I read Camus' Rebel and gave up the idea of god. God, like government, was an impediment and an offense to a mature human being.

Still, the world is a circular place. Ultimately, it is only your own backside blocking the view.

COMING HOME   DAVID WIDUP

Unlike most, I came back home, but didn't get out. I had two more years to serve in the Air Force when I landed at McGuire AFB, New Jersey on a muggy September night in 1970. After depositing two cigarette packs full of "The World's Best Grass" in the Amnesty Box, I took off my jungle fatigues, put them in the trash can and put on the civilian clothes I had bought in Japan the night before, after the first leg of the trip home (Bien Hoa - Yakota, Japan, - Anchorage, Alaska - McGuire). I was clean and sober, but felt hung over and numb. It was a black night, thunderstorms without lightening.

Before going to my next duty station in Wyoming, I had 33 days of leave that started in New York City. I slept all the way to my sisters' apartment, arriving at 3:30 AM. I just sat and looked at them. I didn't know what to say. They seemed strange to me. I felt their anticipation with every breath. I don't remember any conversation, though I know we talked until dawn.

I went to wash my clothes at a Laundromat around the corner the next afternoon and remember feeling ashamed at how stunning and beautiful the young women looked to me. I remember feeling dirty and unworthy. When they looked at me, I felt scorn and shame. It hurt - they were so beautiful and I was so dirty.

Coming home is the hardest part. I've been doing it for almost 25 years and still haven't gotten it right.

DRYING OUT

I am sitting on a beach in Australia.
Scarbourough Beach it's called.
It is winter in the southern hemisphere
so no one is here but Flo and me
and some gulls that will whistle
God Save The Queen for a rancid french-fry.

I've been sitting here for a month.
I carried 90 pounds of books with me.
Before that we left Saigon in a white rage,
then went to Hong Kong and Singapore—
they weren't much fun any more.
When the plane landed in Perth
they sprayed us with bug poison.

Every day I sit on the beach and write.
I do not write about the Nam or war or dying.
I write about gulls, the sea and clouds.
Our flat is a block away and made of brick.
They have left large holes in the walls
for ventilation. Mosquitoes the size of
Cobra gun ships circle my head all night.
They want to suck blood and inject dreams.
There is something that is stalking my dreams—
monsters born from what people do to other people.
Last night I put the mattress on the floor
and pitched the tent on top of it.
They can't get in—nothing can get to me.

I am sitting on a beach in Australia
and the waves keep coming
in like clockwork, pounding the sand,
and rushing out again.
The Indian Ocean is as gray and cold
as an army of lead soldiers
and there are not enough oceans—
there are not enough rivers—
there is not enough rain—
there are not enough tears
in this whole, sad world
to get me clean.

PEACE CORPS PRINCESS
KUALA LUMPUR, 19 JULY 71

The day is not digesting well.
I remember the noodle factory
with clotheslines of drying noodles
flapping in the hot wind
like a cheap curtain in a bad movie.
I remember the fish, slightly rotten.
I remember the heat,
the exhaustion and dehydration.
I can recall my impatience and depression.
I remember a man who wrapped packages
as if it were some kind of an art.
I remember the hungry, the industrious,
the tired and the ambitious.
The massage parlors are not big business yet.
The locals only hate Australians on sight.
The bar girls and the whores
do not have the eyes of combat veterans yet.
The obscene tourists with their busy cameras
and corrosive money haven't arrived here yet.

The people still remember how to smile.

We are eating in a cheap restaurant.
The food is vaguely Chinese and not too bad.
The walls need paint but the geckos are busy.
The air is tropic hot and moonless black.

No one is shooting in the streets.

We are talking and eating with a bunch
of Peace Corps workers from Burma and India.
They are serenely confident, doing the right thing.
They have lived poor, eaten bad, got dysentery,
helped the downtrodden,
and never had a bad day in their lives.

A young girl with rich genes
and flaming self righteousness
accuses me of immorality
for having been a civilian in Saigon.

She is sure that I have personally murdered infants,
burned villages, raped women and tortured prisoners.

She doesn't know a thing about me.
She doesn't know that I have made mistakes
but I have never done a wrong thing twice.
She gets up and says she can't
eat with scum like me.

My stomach goes sour.
I just look down at my hands,
force the tears down the back of my throat.
I can't eat the not too bad Chinese food.
I can't talk anymore.

She is a rich princess bitch and she is right.
She doesn't know that if she is right then she is wrong.
She doesn't know that she is a parasite too.
She doesn't know she squats on the top of a culture
that squats on the top of many less powerful cultures.
She doesn't know that the Peace Corps
is the first step of Imperial conquest.
She doesn't know that she bought the downtrodden
for whitewash to paint over her own guilt.
She doesn't know that we are all guilty.
She doesn't know that only the most successful parasites
can afford guilt, good deeds and indignation.
She doesn't know she is worse than the most brutal soldier.

And she never will.

LOOKING BACK   MICHAEL ANDREWS

A full year after leaving The Nam we came home to The World. It was not any home that I could recognize. We slunk into town like returning exiles still in shame. Except for family and a few friends there was no parade. I never did come home. Ultimately I made a new home in an alien country called the US of A.

There were whole cross sections of previous acquaintances and friends I simply could not talk to. Most Americans were undigestible fast food. They were appallingly ignorant, ethically ambivalent, spoiled rotten, infantile egotists who were at best dangerous, at worst racially suicidal. And, they were fat.

The overwhelming impression of The World was that it was somehow much less than real. It was a ghostlike world populated by pseudo-humans and pod-people. In general they seemed to be more or less exactly the way I later described one of them. "You have the heart of a 105 Howitzer. The mind of a cuckoo clock. The empathy of a cheap pocket calculator. The ethics of a slime mold. Your greatest dreams are trivial. Your deepest thoughts are infantile. Your best conversation is white noise. Your best day is unmemorable. Your greatest deed is a bore. Your most profound suffering is silly. You have the presence of a fart in a hurricane. Your most considered opinion is worth less than a mosquito turd. You have the IQ of a breath mint. And, you are ugly."

I have continued to hold the same opinion of the great mass of humanity ever since.

The World itself had become a Disney Fantasyland because death was not an immediate concern. There were no peak experiences, no pressing intellectual, moral or cultural issues to resolve. Nothing kept the adrenals pumping. The obscurity of death as a factual reality made for an infantile avoidance of hard thinking and mature growth. Everyone lived forever. There was a chicken in every pot, a Ford in every garage. Everyone was fat and happy. Everyone was as dead and dumb as a can of spaghetti.

It took about ten years to look back. When I did, I cried. It finally dawned on me how profoundly The Nam had effected me. I looked back because I was in pain and I was angry and it just plain took ten years to digest the lessons. Nothing in my life had so radically changed me and my thinking so quickly—nothing matched the magnitude and the intensity of it. Other things affected me as deeply, such as being crippled as a child, reading, thinking, art, love and a motorcycle accident. But they were slow, normal kinds of processes and did not involve the rape of other humans.

When I looked back I began to grow nostalgic for The Nam, the place to which so much of my life was tied. I realized that I loved it, the beauty, the people, the monsoons and Buddhas, the jungles and sunsets. I wanted to go back. I began to fear that in that moment when the plane took off and I decided out of anger not to look back at The Nam I had cursed myself to a kind of exile. That I could never go back. And, in truth, I have never been back. Who knows, maybe someday I will.

But I now know that I can never go back to The Nam that was mine even if I did step off a plane at Ton Son Nhut, just the same way that I never came home either. It is a different place now, and probably worse for all the lack of killing. America was not the only culture to die in that dirty little war. And I am not the same either—in some deep sense the child I was born as died in that war too. Still, I like to imagine that just revisiting that geography would let me bury some ghosts that belong to that landscape alone.

Nowadays I live at home as an alien resident in the country of my birth. It is a dying culture, corrupt and decaying at every level. Life gets harder and meaner every day. The national character is coarser, less educated, more venal and even more spoiled. There is desperation in the air, as if the citizens of Pompeii know the volcano is angry. We are taking casualties at an unprecedented rate.

It was a long time from Periclean Athens to Jeffersonian America. Now that it too has fallen I doubt that The World can survive another wait as long. Perhaps for cultures, as for individual humans, events have a way of speeding up and compressing with age, and that some new light of freedom and democracy will be born in some emerging nation.

    Flo and I are still in love and still at war. It turns out that with two well intentioned human beings love does not die after twenty some odd years, it matures. As for me, I am still Diogenes searching for decency, and when I watch the evening news I get profoundly sad, but when I look out the window I am still glad enough to be alive.

MICHAEL ANDREWS

WHAT I LIKE, WHAT I CAN, WHAT IS EASY AND WHAT IS HARD

I get up in the morning, desperate.
When I look into the mirror
and I see desperate eyes
I know I'm living right.

I like men that do desperate things.
I use a cleaver with the authority of a man
who knows a sausage from a porkchop.
I like the wrench in the stomach
when I break laws, smuggle cocaine
climb cliffs, and lie to the IRS.
I like the curling lip of dangerous women
and knives in the boots of desperate men
and running red lights.
I like food that stings,
women that bite, cats that claw,
men that go where other men would not.
It's a matter of spice.
It isn't easy to explain
to people who don't need it,
who ask why I don't do something useful
get a job, pay some tax, make babies.

I say -
I can run, can sing, can laugh.
I can write poems, program a computer.
I can fix plumbing, sail a ship
hope, solve equations, play a guitar.
I can cheat, give, ask, shape wood,
carve stone, take pictures, wait.
I can kill, forgive, steal, grow.
I can wound, heal, be hurt. I can love,
can fuck, can cook, can sew.
I can hate, think, fight, care, sweat.
I can dream, die, dare. I can do anything—
and everything I tell you has some kind of use.

I like men who carry knives in their eyes
whose words cut dangerous,
honed razors in their dreams.
I like women with cheeks that suck in
mean and hungry and dangerous as jaguars.

MICHAEL ANDREWS

I like poems with the power.
I like life where I find it.
And there is just one thing I have to say—
it is easy to go on breathing
but it's hard to stay alive.

THE BOYS

PART 1
They were mostly all different.
They were all the same.
These boys were black and white
and Hispanic and Oriental
and Heintz 57.

And now they think they want to know
about the boys so different from so many places and times.
They were from big towns and small towns
and all the ones in between.
They were from New York, Chicago and LA.
They were from Grand Junction, Colorado,
Joliet, Illinois,
Rockaway, New Jersey,
Snohomish, Washington.
They were off farms,
out of the ghetto,
and from the burbs.

They were stupid, they were smart.
They were TMRs and EMRs,
valedictorians and Rhodes Scholars.
And they were mostly a bunch of boys with 100 IQ.

They were criminals
and addicts
and derelicts
and idiots
and homosexuals
and hucksters.

They were single
married
divorced
gay
and all combinations and permutations thereof.
They were mostly not very much the same.
They were different as different can be.

But the boys were all the same
because the boys were there.
And the boys are diseased.
And some of the boys are dead.
And now they want to know about the boys

DAVID WIDUP

and about their time in the war to forgotten.

So, tell them. Let them know.
Let 'em in on the big secret.
Tell them about the blood and rockets and guns and dung.
Tell them of the acrid smells of sulphur from
guns and rockets going all day and all night.
Tell them of the heat and humidity and how everything,
absolutely everything, rotted. Clothes, food, paper
ammunition, living skin, dead skin - it all rotted
in the unrelenting heat and humidity.

Tell them of the nice boy,
just two weeks in hell,
gone mad - stark raving mad-
with 350 fun filled, action packed days to go
and nowhere to go but down, down, down.

Tell them of the drugs and lies and cheating.
Mescaline, speed, acid, grass, ludes, coke, smack,
booze, hash, reds, greens, yellows, whites -
you name it, the boys got it.
Tell them of the gook whores that sucked up
the boys juices and took their money and
gave them the clap and crabs and gonorrhea,
and sometimes stabbed them in the back—

not a pretty way to go!

Tell them of the boys killing their own
like they killed the others,
just slightly confused about
who the real enemy was.

Tell them about the guards in the tower,
watching the old lady chase after her cow
into the perimeter and how the boys fought like dogs
for the right to blow her away and how the boy
first shot the cow so she knew, really knew,
she was going to eat the big one next
and how he shot with a grin six times and
how they all bragged about it on and on.

Tell them of the "Dear John" letters the boys all got
and how after awhile they were glad to get them
cause they knew they were coming and now
they didn't need to worry about it any more.

The boys thought it must have been great sport
courtin' and fuckin' their girls and wives
cause it just never stopped, it just never stopped.

Tell them about the empty, painful spaces
that grew bigger and bigger and bigger
every Goddamn day and how even the best
tried to fill those spaces with the drugs
and sex and booze and food and violence
and how only by killing or leaving themselves
empty as a can of dead C-rats
did the spaces go away.

Tell them about the worst horror of all—
coming home to nothing.
Nothing at all.
Nothing to be, nothing to do, nothing to say.
Tell them about the boys.
Be specific. Give the fucking details.
Tell the fucking story—
event by image by each sorry moment.

I tried to tell you

You weren't listening.

MICHAEL ANDREWS

THE PLACE WE ARE AT LOOKS LIKE HOME BUT I WAKE UP IN THE MORNING AND THE SHOES DON'T FIT

You will die like a dog for no good reason.
Ernest Hemingway, Notes on the Next War

Rick wanders the deserts and the rivers
looking and looking and looking
and Lance jumps every time a car backfires
and Posty is in the Peten Jungle
looking for a 2000 year old indian man
and Gringo Jim runs a Texaco station in Honduras
and he can't speak a word of spanish
and other friends are in Iran
sweating mules and bleeding flies.
We are looking for a familiar street,
a favorite cafe, the face of the man
that used to sell newspapers or popsicles,
a nickname that a lover used to tease us with
and I guess we are each alone
whether we like it or not
coming back to the World
full of people as solid as
a dream of fog on a windy night,
ghosts on the other side of a river
and sometimes we even talk to you
about ring-around-the-collar
and next year's super bowl
and sometimes we kid ourselves into
thinking that we have come home.

A city is a woman with a million lovers.
I left her alone and when I came back
she had lost my phone and address.
I live in Los Angeles, a city that I left
in 1969—and I never came back.

I wake up in the morning and I know better.
The sign on the freeway says Los Angeles—
it's a trick, like mirrors and Social Security.
I am not someone named Michael Andrews,
number 557-64-5507, and this city
is not Los Angeles, California 90254

and you are not reading this poem.

BACK IN THE WORLD

NEW YORK CITY
The noise hurts my ears
as I walk from my sister's place
in Greenwich Village to Macy's.
I keep turning my head to catch all the sights.
Car horns startle me.
I look into the faces of passing strangers.
They don't meet my gaze,
they turn away.
I wonder, do I smell like Vietnam.
I consider buying a wig.
The policeman doesn't know where Macy's is,
says he's not a tour guide.
Finally, I buy two pairs of jeans,
some cotton shirts and a sweater.
I can't walk all the way back.
The noises fall out of my ears.
My eyes bleed mirrors and sights,
my mouth trembles.
I grab a cab, sweating and
don't leave the apartment for
another three days.

ROCKAWAY, NJ
Bob Koch rolls a thin joint that we smoke.
I drive to the pool hall in Dover and
beat him three games in a row,
worry he lets me win.
The felt is a rust color
that keeps my gaze too long.
"How was it over there?"
I sink into myself,
stunned by the obvious question.
"I grew up a lot".
Bob asks "Could you have grown like that here?"
I can't think the answer through.
My field of vision is just the pool table.
I start shaking,
my stomach returns to its favorite knot,
I tell Bob I need to go.
We drive to his home in silence
His Mom gives me a big hug.
Bob and I don't say good-bye when I leave.

DAVID WIDUP

CHAMPAIGN, IL.
She talks to me non stop for hours,
about school, men, bicycles, the War, Nixon,
the military industrial complex, conformity.
It's much later when she tells me she's engaged,
after her diet and the weather next week.
I fall into myself in silence,
tears run down my throat,
my fingers tremble as I pull a Winston
from the flip top pack and light it.
They sleep together with their clothes on, she says,
and I think about maybe going back to Nam
Life is too weird here.

NORMAN, OK
Dad lives with Rick in Married Student Housing.
They're upset I'm only spending four days with them,
even though I got here two days early,
left Champaign on Saturday, not Sunday,
and drove straight through.
I'm afraid to sleep in a strange bed one more night.
Dad and I drink beer and talk about his studies.
He's decided, he tells me, that maybe Vietnam was wrong,
being back on campus has made him more liberal,
more open minded he thinks.
Vietnam was wrong.
My guts over there on the ground, buddies dead,
soul split open and scrambled,
Vietnam was wrong, he says.
Rick and I play football with some undergrads.
They get tough with Rick,
and on the next play I take them both out in one tackle.
One walks away limping, the other waits for crutches.
I walk back angry that this makes me smile.
I'm glad to head to base the next morning.

THE POW'S SITCOM
8 OCT 79, MONDAY NIGHT.

So here I am in front of the tube
watching Hal Holbrook play this guy Denton.
He wants to thrill us with an epical
saga of being a POW in the Hanoi Hilton.
I am hoping for a cheap John Wayne rip-off
but it turns into hyper-jingoism before
the first commercial break.

When Hell Was In Season they call it
and he plows through most of hell between beer commercials
and the carny bits of news flashes.
The guy takes seven years in a bad hotel,
no food, sleeping in pig shit,
not to mention a regular course of tortures
and all they ask is what kind of plane he flew.

This was a serious guy.
This is a guy with the intellect of a sub-normal stink bug.
I give him A+ for gullibility, credulity
and for being bone stubborn and I toddle off
to take a commercial piss sandwiched
between headache propaganda and sitcom come-ons.

The first thing a sane man does is kick back,
put his feet on the desk and say to the enemy,
"Tell me what you want to know?"
This moron spouts the Bible at his tormentors.
I am sure that a cut-throat bunch of non-practicing Buddhists
were thrilled by chapter and verse
but then apparently these brave lads
nearly destroyed the entire NVA by singing
a stirring, if somewhat ragged,
version of *God Bless America*.

I know that Chistmas time for POWs
in the Hanoi Hilton will certainly move me.
I know I am moved enough to explore the refrigerator
for something more palatable than
infantile patriotism and Peanut Butter ads.

In the end the good Commander does get home,
as all great heroes do.

MICHAEL ANDREWS

His wife has been fucking a vibrator for eight years.
His son has joined the Marines.
The hero gets off the plane
and he doesn't even say, "Hi"—
no Errol Flynn wink, not even a Stan Laurel wave.
No sir, he makes a speech thanking America
and I hit the TV's kill button
just before I am fully informed
about a miracle ingredient that
will kick the living shit out of mud stained socks.

Before plunging into a night of reckless dreams
I sit on the toilet and contemplate war
and the meaning of Mountain Grown Coffee.
I wipe my ass with the Nixon maneuver
and flush my finest into the Pacific.

Commander Denton belongs to history now
and tomorrow I have to find a TV
with a remote control
and study the TV Guide with a bit more care.

THE BARRACKS

The barracks room they've given me
back here in the world
is square cinderblock
with black linoleum floor
and white, painted smooth ceiling.
It's too cold,
so I fill it with rugs
and posters and music and
dope and books and guitars.
I come back from three days
on the missile site and
smoke joints and listen to my friends,
Stills, Clapton, Joni Mitchell.
Scars still soft and bleeding
I sit on the bed smiling,
hoping, through ignorance
and escape, that eventually
things will be OK.

MICHAEL ANDREWS

4DAY TIRE STORE
LOS ANGELES, 12 FEB 92

> "He (the District Chief) told them specifically that if they did not personally see an incident, then it did not occur."
>
> **Gloria Emerson,** Winners & Losers

The rain boils on the pavement
like a sizzling monsoon in a distant jungle
in a war far, far ago.
It wept when it killed our joy there.
It weeps now as we rot
in this stinking, wet desert
while the rich folk scream in their canyons
about mud on the carpets,
rain in the mansion
and rust on the Beamer.

A child sits in the hot, green rain
in that far, far war ago.
Her stomach is an overripe mellon.
Her eyes are as dead as a sun baked trout.
Her legs are broken pencils.
Her clothes would not survive a modest washing.
Her death doesn't make a sound
as it falls in the forest of broken lives.
No one hears her final sigh,
so no one asks if a someone really died
until the rain boiled the pavement today

and I looked out the window.

COMBAT BOOTS

These canvas topped, black leather, GI issue boots
have steel plates in molded rubber soles
to protect me from the curse
of punji sticks, shit tipped bamboo that
will kill from the bottom up.
I lived in these boots, night and day,
they became an extension of my body,
an appendage to my feet.

The circular metal air holes on the instep
closest to my balls, a disk of copper
and pinholes for feet to breathe like lungs
is a new orifice for me,
another hole to fill with something, anything,
a new emptiness for strange tongues to
dance across in dreams on drunken, lonely nights with
pits that have no bottom to explore before
the dawn that slides, then cracks, then slams
into my eyes like a C5A,
landing at Cam Rahn Bay, sliding over the
tarmac, AM2 matting and into the sand
and sinking so far it takes a month to pull it out.

My boots smell like rotten jungle in the closet.
I will not throw them out; I'll keep them with me.

PATCHES

We're sitting in Conference Room C,
fifteen of us around four rectangular tables
of white formica with oak trim on the edges
arranged to make an even bigger rectangle,
the four corners in the middle not quite the same height,
so it looks more like a volcano
than a small white plain.
We're here to learn to solve problems together,
my associates and I,
on this warm, sunny late fall day in LA,
and I'm hoping my problems can be solved,
and don't think too much about my other work today.

To break the ice,
we take turns talking about ourselves.
We state our name, job and
something about ourselves
the others are not likely to know.
It's already sounding strangely like
name, rank, serial number and date of birth.
My companions are a boring, predictable bunch.
One plays basketball,
another's an ocean swimmer
and another coaches kid's soccer.
The Pakistani plays classical guitar
and the Spaniard plays the flute.
I'm the next to last to go
and tell them my name, job
and that I'm a musician -
a 12 string blues guitarist.
I don't tell them I'm a poet,
after all, I work with these jerks.

The last to go is Mel.
His big secret is that
he does volunteer work with his son
through the church, and now
they are focused on our servicemen in the Middle East,
sending packages and, more importantly he says,
letters to Americans in the Gulf,
and they've already received some of the things
he and his son have sent,
and one of the servicemen over there even
sent a letter back to his son
(and by now, old Mel's chest is really full,

he's proud and strutting his stuff!)
and, he adds, his son even got a patch
from this serviceman who wrote back
after getting a package with their letter in it.

I'm deaf now,
and watch Mel's lips move
with no sound coming out.
He's smiling and there's
a distinctive sharpness in his gaze
as he talks to the seminar leader
at the other end of the four table rectangle,
and it's way too big now,
longer than a football field,
larger even than the rice paddy,
just south of Tuy Hoa;
way too big to be in this room.

Without thinking,
I stand up so quick
I knock my chair over,
and grab Mel by the nape of the neck,
slam the side of his head into the formica.
His mouth opens,
his eyes roll back in his head
and his alcoholic red cheeks turn white,
but I feel a strong pulse
in the palm of my right hand.
He's not dead.

And where the fuck were you
on December 25th, 1968
Mr. Mel!?!?!?
Where the fuck were you
and your God damned
cards, letter and packages?
When I was alone and crazy in RVN,
where was all your religious,
1990s caring bullshit?
And why,
dear God in heaven, why
are you so proud of
your son's patch?

Patches tell where we belong,
which company, which division.
We wear them even in the field,

DAVID WIDUP

it's the only thing on our jungle fatigues,
even our God damned, worthless rank
is missing from our armor -
but not our patch -
it tells us where we belong,
it allows the lifers to keep us
in line, in formation, in our death place,
it's our prison
right there
on our left shoulder
for all the world to see.

We put our patches
in the mouths of whores
and on the bodies
of our dead buddies.
I'm ripping the patch
from my shoulder,
my hand shaking bad,
pulling my nails away from the quick,
pulling, tugging
until it pulls free
in my bloody fingers
and I throw it in Mel's face
and it sticks there.

My lips are just a hair breath away from Mel's ear.
I'm screaming now.
We smoke dope in patches.
They go places
in the dead and dying
no son of yours belongs!
Your son got a patch!
Tell him to burn it,
throw it away.
It will do him no good,
it's bad luck.
Patches aren't meant for young boys
who go to church with Dad
on Sunday mornings and fill packages
with Girl Scout cookies and letters
for our soldiers in the Gulf.
Mail it to your Congressman
and have him take it to the Wall.
Patches. Jesus H. Christ!

On December 25th, 1968,

I sat alone in
a hot, wet connex bunker
on the south perimeter
of a small compound
on the Black Virgin Mountain
called Nuy Bah Dihn.
I had been there, awake
for several days and nights.
We had all been real aware it was Christmas.
There was no shuckin and jivin,
no "Don't mean nothin",
no "Screw it, it don't matter"
that day - it was bad quiet.
The sky was blue black with
sharp stars and it was way too warm
to be Christmastime.
I had been nowhere for a very long time
with my 823rd CES Red Horse buddies.

What I wanted for Christmas
was a soft, warm breast
to rest my face against,
a strong hand
gently touching my temple
stroking my pain away,
taking the weight in my chest
somewhere else.

But alone, with wet feet,
I would have killed,
I mean killed,
for a box of Girl Scout cookies
and a friendly letter
from a strange kid
in Yorba Linda, California.
None came,
but we did anyway.

BETWEEN A PIG AND A BABY

There is a soldier on a boat in a sea of pain and the sea is called Vietnam.
He is rescuing people in a flood. The monsoons come and kill people like butterflies in a jar of formaldehyde. The soldier feels good. He is saving instead of killing—a moment of peace in an ocean of murder.
On every boat there is a policeman and the law. The policeman only allows each victim to bring one thing on the boat when they pull them out like human sardines. It is the only way to save lives and not sink the boat. So that is the law.
Even good will is bound by sweet necessity.
The old mamasan is nearly drowned. She is in the water up to her neck, treading away her last bit of life. She has rescued a baby and a pig. It is everything she has left in life.
And the boat to life is full. It always is. The soldier pulls it along side, glad to be of help. The cop is a cop and so he is a sadist. He won't pull her in unless she only has one "thing."
They argue for a while, but the cop likes the law better than he likes people, so mamasan pushes the infant under the swirling flood. She holds it down until it stops thrashing. She lets it go and it bobs to the surface like a sad cork drifting with the current, searching for a bottle to plug.
The policeman pulls mamasan into the boat, laughing. Mamasan sits staring at the horizon, that place where the sea meets the sky, and clutches her pig. She just needs that pig, you see.

The soldier is never the same after that.
After that, life never means what it is commonly held to mean.

It's like this—to save your faith in human kind you can choose to believe that maybe the infant wasn't hers. Maybe.
You can rescue your grip on sanity by understanding that infants in Vietnam rarely lived beyond three years. Hell, they don't even name them until they're five. That baby was going to die no matter what.
You can redeem your little card house of ethical cliches by clutching to the sad fact that babies were easier to come by than a decent meal—the plain fact is that there were too many mouths to feed already.
You can keep your last fantasy of common decency by grasping the grim truth that without that pig both mamasan and the baby would soon starve to death. This way, at least, two lives trudged on down that road with no scenic vistas, without a single rest stop, without roadsigns or miles-to-go or direction of travel, without maps or destination or meaning, and certainly, without love. The Vietnamese even have a street named for life—it is called the Street Without Joy.
The bottom line is that she needed that pig.
Even horror, you see, has its own terrible kind of logic.

I urinate six ways on logic. Fuck facts—I know better.

It is merely what war and law and sometimes life does to people. It freezes their hearts into little blocks of snot and cinder. The blood still pumps through their veins, but their real hearts float away in the currents of that stupid and brutal flood of tears.

I ought to know. Thirty years later I row a boat in a sea of pain. Desperate lives come floating to me and I haul them into the boat and tell them we are sailing to an island of joy and laughter. It is a harmless little fantasy. I know that we can't help anyone really. Hell, we can barely keep ourselves afloat. Mostly we drown quietly in that sea of human tears. So it is my own little illusion to get me through the night, trying to help people. I know it's impossible. But I keep on trying. I need that illusion.
Lance and I grew up in the same crib. But life just chipped him down to a naked skeleton, exposed nerves and an empty stomach. The doctors proclaimed paranoia and manic depression and got rich on the pills that ate his mind away. Lance just needs to be a normal guy. All he gets is thrown out of restaurants. Lance has lost his mind and he knows it. He needs a friend. All he gets is bartenders. He wants love. All he gets is toleration. Lance is crazy. Lance is lost. I am his last link to a world that is floating away.
Flo's sister Anita is crazy in her own style. She is mean and terrified and she has starved the meat off her bones like an old lady poster for Auschwitz. The bulimia has eaten away her power to think, to love, to grasp any other world but her tiny life of pain and fear sweating beneath an empty sky.
One day I haul one too many out of that sea and the boat just sinks. I am out of time and money and strength. Pain and death just eat holes in the bottom of the boat and leave me treading water in the flood. We starve to death that way, eating other people's pain. Pain has no calories, no fat, no protein, not a single vitamin, and it's completely mineral free.

Eating other people's pain is life's little Twinky, just empty calories—in an hour, or maybe two, you're starving again.

My cousin Chris is a 44-year-old infant. She has two little girls that are older than she has ever been. She would sell them down any kind of river for a single Quaalude. She has eaten her own heart with downers and uppers and credit cards. She has an army of drug pushers whose names always end with the initials "M.D." One child is autistic from in utero drug abuse. The other is stunted from neglect and poor nutrition. Chris needs that drug. Her husband needs to take the kids, sell the house, get a divorce and dump Chris into the nearest sewer. He has had enough. He is taking the children and swimming for the boat. He just needs that pig.

The phone rings—what can we do? how can we save Chris? I grab that load of pain and swim with one good arm.

MICHAEL ANDREWS

My brother Rick was in Vietnam. He saw things so horrible that he has crawled into a bottle and has taken twenty years to drown. He did things in Nam that make ghosts stalk him in his dreams. He can't hold still for fear of memory. He had a friend, Russell, whose name he can only mention when we are deep into the desert alone with the wind and the sky and the horizon. Russell and he were driving in a truck for Ben Het. A mine turned Russell into a little glob of bloody snot and crispy cinder. Russell lived with that fact for three days and then floated off with the current.

Rick's life is in the toilet. The alcohol is eating his health. He only sleeps three hours a night. His wife has left him. He got arrested for a felony break-in when he was in a drunken rage. He is about to lose his job. He calls me on the phone and adds his tears to that flood of human misery. He is alone. I don't mean the kind of alone you get on an empty Saturday night—I mean the kind of alone you get when you open the closet and all you find is empty hangars.

Rick is my little brother. He is as sweet and innocent and loving as anyone who ever walked this street without joy. I can't imagine trudging down that road without him. I need Rick so I can hang on to my little fantasy of life. I take hold and kick against the current. Rick is my pig and Chris is my baby. Somewhere out here there there has to be a passing boat.

When it comes it has a policeman and the law and it's full right up to the gunnels. I don't know what you'd do, and I don't care—you figure it out. I need that pig.

I drown the baby—and get on board.

WHISPERING AT THE WALL

The black polished wall
gleams even in the dark
after the lights are put out.
Lincoln, perched stiffly
in his huge chair is
reflected against the names
of the boys killed in 1967,
between June and July -
a whole panel of names -
it was a deadly summer.

She is dressed in a long, red winter coat,
a stocking cap, black gloves and tall boots,
her cheek and palms pressed against the Wall,
she's whispering so quietly even she cannot hear.
Her lips never stop moving
except when she
bends down a little,
from time to time,
and kisses a name,
the same name
all night long.
She whispers mutely with hands
pressed against the Wall
the way a woman puts her hands
on her man's chest,
and bends and kisses
just below Lincoln's beard
reflected against the black, hard granite,
and keeps on
whispering at the Wall.

WARS, BLOODY WARS

Now that they think they need to know,
they smell the blood, see the pain again
of the boys and their beating black sorrow.

Fields on fire, skies yellow in napalm glow,
render tired eyes wet, cracked glasses fall from gold rims,
now that they think they need to know.

Letters from home, an acid hard undertow,
etch lines deep into hard faces too thin
of the boys and their beating black sorrow.

Fish smelling whores who hurt when they blow
take God far away, but black out the coffin,
now that they think they need to know.

Eyes, black, gone vacant mad like a scarecrow,
hard barbs stay deep under pale skin
of the boys and their beating black sorrow.

Wars, bloody wars, the people all bellow,
afraid the next body bag will be kin,
now that they think they need to know
of the boys and their beating black sorrow.

THINGS THAT BREAK

Ship Ahoy your baby boy is home from Vietnam. **John Prine**

I am eating a chili dog in the Pier Sandwich Shop.
FOOD TO GO it says in mirror
image on the inside of the window.

I look out at Pier Avenue.
The traffic never lets up;
cars and bodies and bikinis and dogs and roller skates.
I am thinking about things that break;
clocks and volkswagons
marriages
and glass.

The curious thing about glass
is that it comes two ways—
windows and mirrors.
Windows make you free.

Mirrors let you know.

I got my first wrinkle in Vietnam.
In Nicaragua the bullets fluttered like gnats
and the gray hairs sprouted on my chest
like a cash crop.

I am watching the people go by on Pier Avenue.
I don't know who they talk to.
I don't know what they talk about.
When I get my second chili dog
with mustard and onions
some old lady says that it's
because the food is so good.

Conversation, I guess.

I don't say a thing.
I don't know what to tell her.
I remember jungle and heat and rain
like Noah never dreamed
and I think—

No, lady, there is something empty
way down here.

MICHAEL ANDREWS

What have they got to talk about?

What I want to say is that I hurt.
The world on the other side of that glass **hurt me**
and I am thinking about things that **break**
mirrors and minds
windows and backs.

Some of them were friends of mine.

Don't ever
Don't ever
Don't ever
send me to another war.
Don't send my friends.
Don't send my children.
Don't tell me any goddamn reason
for any goddamn
bullet.

Next time
I'll know who to kill.

I eat my chili dog
looking out the window.

FOOD TO GO.

I damn near cried
on a perfectly beautiful day.

MICHAEL ANDREWS

is co-founder/publisher/editor with Jack Grapes of Bombshelter Press and ONTHEBUS, living, for the moment, in L.A. and getting by. He has published 7 books of poetry, and 3 fine print poetry/photography portfolios. He has traveled around the world twice, spent time in Vietnam and Iran, rode a motorcycle to Peru, ran the San Juan River and recently spent a month in the Peruvian Amazon. His leg was seriously damaged in a motocycle accident in 1987. He is currently working on two novels, a book of speculative philosophy, and creating photographic and poetry montages as digital images. He works as a computer programmer/analyst. He worked as a civilian in Vietnam from 1969 through 1971.

DAVID WIDUP

was born in Riverside, California: now resides in L.A. county and in between has lived in seventeen places including four foreign countries — the most foreign of which was Vietnam. He has co-authored a book of poetry with Stellasue Lee, *Over To You* (Bombshelter Press), and is a production manager for ONTHEBUS. From September 18, 1969 to September 20, 1970 David served in Vietnam with 823rd CES (Red Horse) in many locations including Bien Hoa, Cam Ranh Bay, Phan Rang, Nuy Bha Dinh and Pleiku.